WALKER'S CO~

YORKSHIRE DALES

WALKER'S COMPANION

YORKSHIRE DALES

FRANK DUERDEN

Photography by David Ward

WARD LOCK

ACKNOWLEDGMENTS

The preparation of this book, including the original edition, has taken up most of my spare time over a total period of about two years. It has been made considerably easier and certainly far more enjoyable by the kindness and help that I have received from many people, most of whom live in the Dales area. In particular, I thank the staff of the Yorkshire Dales National Park Authority who gave a great deal of their time to ensure that my manuscript was accurate and as up-to-date as possible. Mr T. Harper formerly of Ghyll Farm, Sedbergh read through the section on farming and Dr. Yvonne Williams of The Polytechnic of North London, helped me with the sections on the geology. I have to thank the Countryside Commission for permission to include the Countryside Access Charter. Some information has been included from the initial National Park Plan. The maps were drawn from 1:25 000 maps with the permission of the Ordnance Survey. Finally, I must thank Mrs. Jennifer Peck and my daughters, Beverley and Sharon, for typing the manuscripts, and my wife, Audrey, who helped me with proof-reading.

A WARD LOCK BOOK
First published in the UK in 1994 by
Ward Lock, Villiers House, 41/47 Strand, London WC2N 5JE

A Cassell Imprint

Text © Frank Duerden 1994   Photographs © Ward Lock 1994

This book is based on material originally published in the *Great Walks* series.

British Library Cataloguing in Publication Data
A cataloguing record for this book is available from the British Library

ISBN 0 7063 7248 4

Typeset by M & R Computerised Typesetting Ltd, of Grimsby, South Humberside

Printed and bound in Spain by Graficromo S.A., Cordoba

All the photographs for this book were taken by David Ward,
except the front cover photograph, which was taken by Archie Miles

CONTENTS

INTRODUCTION

I consider myself very fortunate to have spent my early years in Nelson, a textile town on the extreme northern edge of the Lancashire industrial belt. For not only did it possess an extremely fine cricket team but it also lay within easy reach of the moors of the central and northern Pennines.

As Nelson is a mere 11 miles from the southern boundary of what is now the Yorkshire Dales National Park—the Park was not designated until 1954—visits there, even in those car-less days, were made at frequent intervals. Malham, Gordale, Hawes, Settle and Ingleton have been well-known and well-loved places for as long as I can remember, and the three peaks of Ingleborough, Pen-y-ghent and Whernside found a place on my list of favourite mountains from the beginning.

There are approximately 1100 miles (1770 km) of public footpaths and bridleways within the area of the Park. Those who know the area well will appreciate that it was not an easy task to select nineteen routes which give excellent walking, which are representative of the diverse countryside of the Dales, which offer a range of difficulty and length for walkers of differing ability, which give—on clear days—some of the finest views, which visit some of the most interesting places within the Park, and finally which are free of any access problems. In some cases an excellent walk was omitted because, at the moment, there is some doubt about access. Whether we like it or not, walkers do not have the right to walk anywhere they wish within the National Park and some farmers quite correctly object to walkers crossing their land, away from public footpaths, without permission.

I have been very fortunate during the preparation of this edition, in working with a photographer, David Ward, who obviously sees the Dales in the same way that I do. If, eventually, in extreme old age, my memory does begin to slip away, his superb photographs will, I am sure, bring the beauty of the Yorkshire Dales back to me with all its present clarity.

FRANK DUERDEN

THE YORKSHIRE DALES NATIONAL PARK

John Dower defined a National Park as 'an extensive area of beautiful and relatively wild country in which, for the nation's benefit and by appropriate national decision and action, (a) the characteristic landscape beauty is strictly preserved, (b) access and facilities for public open-air enjoyment are amply provided, (c) wild life and buildings and places of architectural and historic interest are suitably protected, while (d) established farming use is effectively maintained.'

Under the National Parks and Access to the Countryside Act of 1949 a National Parks Commission was established which was responsible for the creation of National Parks; ten were created by the Commission in England and Wales between 1950 and 1957. In 1968 the National Parks Commission was replaced by the Countryside Commission which thereupon took over responsibility for the Parks. A further change came under the Local Government Act of 1972; under this Act a separate National Park Authority was set up for each National Park charged with its administration. Each Authority was given the task of producing a National Park Plan by 1st April, 1977, and of reviewing the plan at intervals of not more than five years. This set out the policies of the Authority for the management of its Park and proposals for carrying out those policies.

The National Park Authorities are charged with two main aims: to preserve and enhance the natural beauty of the areas designated as National Parks; and to encourage the provision or improvement of facilities for the enjoyment of open-air recreation and the study of nature within the National Parks. The Authorities must in addition have due regard for the social and economic needs of the people living and working within them.

It cannot be too strongly emphasized that the area covered by a Park is not 'acquired' by the nation. In the Yorkshire Dales National Park, for example, less than one per cent of the area is under any form of public ownership, the rest is owned and used by private farmers and landowners.

The Yorkshire Dales National Park Committee acts as local planning authority for the area and in that it is no different from

7

Key:
- National Park Boundary
- Road
- Village and town

FIGURE 1 The
Yorkshire Dales
National Park. The
map shows the
boundary, main towns
and villages, and the
more important roads
within and around the
area of the Park.

other local planning authorities throughout England and Wales. Generally, it seeks to work by agreement and co-operation with local owners and occupiers, using compulsory powers only when these fail. Even these compulsory powers are limited in their scope. In the end therefore the Committee relies to a high degree on the goodwill of others.

The overall management of the Park is the responsibility of the Yorkshire Dales National Park Committee. This has twenty-four members, of which twelve are County Councillors of the North Yorkshire County Council, one is a County Councillor of Cumbria County Council, three are District Councillors from the Craven, Richmondshire and South Lakeland District Councils and eight are appointed by the Secretary of State for the Environment (after consultation with the Countryside Commission).

The Committee acts through a team of full-time and part-time staff headed by the National Park Officer. Two Assistant

FIGURE 2 The
principal dales of the
National Park area.

National Park Officers are responsible for the working of offices
at Bainbridge in Wensleydale and Grassington in Wharfedale. A
Head Warden and six Area Wardens are supported in their work
by a number of voluntary wardens.

National Park Centres, which will provide information to
visitors, are at:

Aysgarth Falls   Wensleydale (0969) 663 424
Clapham   Clapham (052 42) 514 19
Grassington   Grassington (0756) 752 774
Hawes   Wensleydale (0969) 667 450
Malham   Airton (0729) 830 363
Sedbergh   Sedbergh (053 96) 20125

These are open April-October inclusive. Opening times do
vary to some extent from year to year and from centre to
centre, but generally they are open daily during this period. There
are also a number of information points through the park.

Those interested in acting as guides on programmed walks or
as voluntary wardens should contact the National Park Office at
Grassington.

9

SOME FACTS AND FIGURES ABOUT THE YORKSHIRE DALES NATIONAL PARK

DESIGNATED 1954. The Park was the seventh of the ten Parks to be designated.

AREA 680 square miles (176 119 hectares). It is the third largest; only the Lake District and Snowdonia National Parks are larger.

EMBLEM Approximately one eighth of this is in Cumbria, the rest is in North Yorkshire.

POPULATION The head of a Swaledale tup (ram). The design was based upon a photograph of the best tup at Muker Show in 1974.

WHERE VISITORS COME FROM (%) There are approximately 18,000 people living within the area of the Park.

England	Day trips	Holidays
Yorkshire/Humberside	65	32
North-West	16	17
Northern	16	12
East Midlands	1	6
South-East	0.5	16
East Anglia	0.3	4
West Midlands	0.2	5
South-West	0.1	2
Scotland	0.6	3
Wales	0.4	2
Overseas	0	1

About eight million people visit the National Park each year; some 90 per cent of these stay for less than six hours.

SELECTED WALKS IN THE YORKSHIRE DALES NATIONAL PARK

Introduction to the Route Descriptions

1. ACCESS
(see page 123)
The majority of walks are along paths for which there is public right-of-way, or which cross moors covered by a current access agreement. Six cross private ground where access is allowed on payment of a small fee (these are indicated). In addition to these, one or two routes have been included to which the above does not apply, but which have, as far as is known, been walked for a long time without objection and it is not expected therefore that difficulties will be encountered. Nevertheless, responsibility must rest with the walker in such cases to obtain any appropriate permission before commencing a walk. 'Short cuts' that might lead to proliferation of paths or to the annoyance of local people should not be taken. Paths are sometimes diverted officially by the National Park Authority, for example to allow a badly-eroded path to recover. The diversion will usually be well-marked. In such cases, of course, the diversion should always be followed.

2. ASCENT
The amount of climbing involved in each route has been estimated from Outdoor Leisure or 1:50 000 maps as appropriate and should be regarded as approximate only.

3. CAR-PARKS
The nearest public car-park is given. There will be many places where a car can be parked by the wayside, but it must be done with care, as indiscriminate parking can be a great nuisance to local people.

4. INTERESTING FEATURES
The best position for seeing these is indicated both in the route descriptions and on the maps by *(1), (2),* etc.

5. LENGTH
These are strictly 'map miles' estimated from the Outdoor Leisure or 1:50 000 maps; no attempt has been made to take into account any ascent or descent involved.

6. MAPS
The maps are drawn to a scale of approximately 1:25 000 (see page 13) and all names are as given on the Outdoor Leisure maps. Field boundaries in particular, which can be a mixture of

Fence	Clear and continuous footpath
Hedge	Intermittent or faint footpath
Wall (intact)	Route over open ground (no footpath)
Wall (broken)	Farm or forest road (not metalled).
Contours (all heights in metres)	Ordnance Survey obelisk
Crag	Cairn
Limestone pavement	Marshy ground
Buildings	Coniferous wood
Stream	Deciduous wood
River (with bridge)	Railway — cutting, embankment, viaduct

Metalled roads indicated by direction arrows

0 _____ 1 miles
0 _____ 1 kilometres

FIGURE 3 *Signs used on maps*

hedge, fence and wall, should be taken as a 'best description'. The maps have been drawn in the main, so that the route goes from the bottom to the top of a page. This will enable the reader to 'line up' the map in the direction walked whilst still holding the book in the normal reading position. The arrow on each map points to grid north. The scale of some small features has been slightly exaggerated for clarity. For easy cross-reference, the relevant Outdoor Leisure and Landranger sheets are indicated on each map.

7. ROUTE DESCRIPTION

The letters 'L' and 'R' stand for left and right respectively. Where these are used for changes of direction then they imply a turn of about 90° when facing in the direction of the walk. 'Half L' and 'half R' indicate a half-turn, i.e. approximately 45°, and 'back half L' or 'back half R' indicate three quarter-turns, i.e. about 135°. PFS stands for 'Public Footpath Sign', PBS for 'Public Bridleway Sign' and OS for 'Ordnance Survey'.

To avoid constant repetition, it should be assumed that all stiles and gates mentioned in the route description are to be crossed (unless there is a specific statement otherwise).

8. STANDARD OF THE ROUTES

The briefest examination of the route descriptions that follow will show that the routes described cover an enormous range of both length and of difficulty; the easiest can probably be undertaken by a family party at almost any time of the year whilst the hardest are only really suitable for experienced fell-walkers who are both fit and well-equipped. Any walker therefore who is contemplating following a route should make sure before starting that it is within his or her ability.

It is not easy in practice however to give an accurate picture of the difficulty of any route, because it is dependent upon a number of factors and will in any case vary considerably from day to day with the weather. Any consideration of weather conditions must, of course, be left to the walker himself (but read the section on safety first). Apart from that, it is probably best to attempt an overall assessment of difficulty based upon the length, amount of ascent and descent, problems of route-finding and finally, upon the roughness of the terrain.

Each of the routes has therefore been given a grading based upon a consideration of these factors and represented by the bold numerals which precedes each walk title. A general description of each grade follows:

Easy (1) Generally short walks (up to 5 miles, 8 km) over well-defined paths, with no problems of route-finding. Some climbing may be involved, but mostly over fairly gradual slopes with only short sections of more difficult ground.

Moderate (2) Rather longer walks (up to about 10 miles, 16 km), mostly over paths, but with sections where route-finding will be more difficult. Mountain summits may be reached with climbing over steeper and rougher ground.

More strenuous (3) Perhaps longer walks (10–20 miles, 16–32 km) with prolonged spells of climbing. Some rough ground, calling for good route-finding ability, perhaps with stretches of scrambling.

FIGURE 4 Starting points. The numbers indicate the starting points for the selected walks described later.

The walks are arranged in order of increasing difficulty, so that Route 1 is the easiest and Route 19 the hardest.

A summary of each walk is given at the head of each section with information on length, amount of climbing and any special difficulties, such as scrambling, that will be met along the way.

9. STARTING AND FINISHING POINTS

With one exception all the routes are circular, returning to their starting point, as this avoids any problems with transport when the walk is completed. The location of each starting point is given by the number of the appropriate Landranger (1:50 000) map with a six figure grid reference (see page 124); thus (98-900627) indicates grid reference 900627 which can be found on Landranger sheet no. 98.

10. TIME FOR COMPLETION

The usual method of estimating the length of time needed for a walk is by Naismith's Rule; 'For ordinary walking allow one hour for every 3 miles (5 km) and add one hour for every 2000 feet (600 m) of ascent; for backpacking with a heavy load allow one hour for every $2\frac{1}{2}$ miles (4 km) and one hour for every 1500 feet (450 m) of ascent'. However, for many this tends to be over-optimistic and it is better for each walker to form an assessment of his own performance over one or two walks. Naismith's Rule also makes no allowance for rest or food stops or for the influence of weather conditions.

1·1

TO MALHAM COVE

STARTING AND FINISHING POINT
Malham National Park Centre car-park (98-900627)

LENGTH
2 miles (3 km)

ASCENT
200 feet (60 m)

The Cove, a magnificent and overhanging precipice 240 feet (73 m) high is one of the most impressive sights in the Yorkshire Dales. It provided the inspiration for Charles Kingsley's *The Water Babies* and in more recent years has been the scene of some of the most difficult and exposed climbs on British limestone. The route from Malham to the Cove along the west side of Malham Beck is very popular, the return over pastures to the east is quieter and better.

ROUTE DESCRIPTION (Map 1)

Leave the large car-park in Malham *(1)* turning L down the minor road past the Information Centre. At the road turn L again and walk to the stone bridge at the centre of the village. Do not cross the bridge, but continue on the road ahead (signpost to Malham Tarn, Langcliffe and Settle). A few yards along, after the telephone box, turn R and then immediately L through a small gate (PFS 'Pennine Way'); this leads to a short but delightful path by the river which is a much better alternative to the road itself. Further along rejoin the road and continue in the same direction. After about 500 yards (460 m) from the bridge in Malham, pass a farmhouse on your R; here the road begins to climb steeply (road sign '1:7 single track road with passing places'). Follow the road up the hill; 175 yards (160 m) after a barn on the R go through a small gate in the wall to the R (Pennine Way sign).

Near Malham Cove. The walk returns to Malham along the opposite side of the stream.

The great cliff of Malham Cove can now be seen directly ahead. Follow the very clear path which heads directly for the Cove. The path crosses a wall at a small gate and then heads slightly R to the bank of the stream. Pass a footbridge, cross a second wall and continue along the bank to reach the cliff at its centre where the stream emerges *(2)*. There are very few places within the Yorkshire Dales — or indeed anywhere, for that matter — more impressive than this spot at the foot of the Cove.

You can return from here by the same route, but it is much better instead to use a footpath on the opposite side of the stream. Cross the stream and walk down on the other bank to a

17

small gate (PFS 'Malham $\frac{3}{4}$'). (When there is too much water to make the crossing, use the footbridge lower down.) At the small gate do not go to the footbridge, but instead go on a path slightly L, soon climbing up a bank (yellow waymarks). At the top continue in the same direction with the steep slope of the bank to your R. Pass to the R of a ruined barn and then follow a wall to a ladder stile in a corner *(3)*. Cross the next field to a gate. Continue in the same direction to a PFS 'Malham/The Cove') and then to the L of a ruined (but substantial) wall, to a further ladder stile. Go between walls (PFS) and then half R across a narrow field to a gate by a small shed in the far L-hand corner (PFS 'Malham/The Cove'). Enter a walled lane and follow it back to Malham, reaching the village by the Youth Hostel.

1 Malham

The exact derivation of the name Malham is not clear, but it may mean 'stony or gravelly place', a name which would be in keeping with much of its surrounding area. In the Domesday Book the name is given as 'Malgun' whilst thirteenth century records show it as 'Malghum' or 'Malgum'. In any event there has been a settlement at Malham for well over one thousand years and human habitation in the area for perhaps three thousand. Today it is without doubt the most popular village in the National Park with one million visitors each year; partly because it is within easy reach of the large industrial towns to the south and east and partly because it is near to three of the most impressive features of the Dales, the Cove, the Tarn and Gordale Scar.

The present bridge which marks the centre of the village is eighteenth century but incorporates much of an earlier pack-horse bridge of the seventeenth, while there are three clapper bridges of earlier origin. The Buck Inn is comparatively recent, but Lister's Arms bears the date 1723. Beck Hall by the road to the Cove is Tudor. The Youth Hostel is one of a chain of hostels along the Pennine Way and the largest in the Park.

2 Malham Cove

The Middle Craven Fault, running roughly east to west just north of Malham, marks the southern limit of the Great Scar Limestone, for the land to the south of it is of a very different character. The Cove and the valley in front of it were created when glacial melt waters ran down the steep hillside produced by the fault and eroded back cutting into the edge of the limestone bed. It is a magnificent sight: a great natural

Opposite *Malham Cove*

amphitheatre with sheer — and, in parts, overhanging — walls tapering back into the hillsides on each side. The stream of icy water issuing from its foot sank underground at Smelt Mill Sink about $1\frac{1}{2}$ miles (2.5 km) to the north-west. As at Gordale Scar house martins build their nests each year under the great overhangs and the birds are a familiar sight in June wheeling and swooping over the huge face.

Magnificent as it may still be, the Cove has, in fact, lost a little of its glory over the years, for the depression in the centre of the cliff was originally the lip of a waterfall, about three times higher than any existing fall in the Dales today. Not since the early years of the nineteenth century however has any water been known to flow over it.

To the rock climber the Cove is the finest crag in the Dales, with about one hundred routes up to 600 feet (180 m) in length. The huge and very impressive Central Wall, directly above the stream exit, was first climbed in 1959.

3 *Iron-Age field boundaries*

The first two fields after leaving the road on the walk to Malham Cove are crossed by a series of parallel ridges running down the hillside towards the stream. These are the remains of Iron-Age field boundaries probably worked about the third century AD. Similar remains can be found at other sites in the Dales.

1·2

AYSGARTH FALLS

After Malham and Bolton Abbey the falls at Aysgarth probably attract more visitors than any other place within the National Park. Due to the difficulties of crossing the river it is probably better to visit the Upper Falls separately. The longer walk to the Middle and Lower Falls can be extended to Castle Bolton if time is available.

ROUTE DESCRIPTION (Map 2)

Upper Falls: Leave the car-park at the opposite end from the road on a path which descends to the L. By the bridge and road go through a small gate and at a kiosk pay a small fee to view the Upper Falls from the river bank. Return by the same route. The best view of the Upper Falls can be obtained from the road bridge *(1) (2)*.

Middle and Lower Falls: Walk from the car-park into the road and turn R. Where the road bends R go L along a path (PFS 'Middle Force/Lower Force'). The Middle Falls can best be seen

STARTING AND FINISHING POINT
Aysgarth Falls car-park and National Park Centre (98-012888). Travelling from Hawes along the A684 turn L about ½ mile (800 m) after Aysgarth, the car-park is on the L soon after a bridge.

LENGTH
Upper Falls: ¾ mile (1.2 km). Middle and Lower Falls: 3 miles (5 km)

ASCENT
Upper Falls: 50 feet (15 m). Middle and Lower Falls: 100 feet (30 m)

from the viewing platform at the side of the path. For the Lower Falls, continue along the path to the L of the river through a wood eventually reaching a small gate; beyond continue to a gate where a descent can be made down a path on the R to the river. The Lower Falls are nearby *(1)*.

After viewing, return to the stile and start to walk back towards the small gate. About half-way along at a PFS ('Aysgarth/Castle Bolton') turn back half R and follow a footpath (marked by yellow waymarks) to a stile. Cross the next field to a gate and then on to the farm just ahead (Hollin House). Go through a stile by a gate to the L of a building and follow the farm road through the farm. Go through the gate by the last building and about 100 yards (90 m) later branch half R at a junction to follow a fence. At a wall go over a stile and continue in approximately the same direction *(3)* to the far corner of the field.

Do *not* go through the gate in the corner but turn back half L and follow the wall *(4)* — i.e. the boundary of the field. Eventually reach a road and follow this — later between walls — to a junction. Go L and after about 50 yards (45 m) turn R over a stile. Follow the wall on the L (i.e. alongside the road) to another stile. Continue in the same direction, descending, as the wall swings away, to a further stile by a gate, then on through yet another stile and then a small gate. Finally, go down some steps into the car-park *(4)*.

1 *The Aysgarth Falls*

The Falls are caused by resistant limestone beds of the Yoredale Series outcropping in the floor of the valley through which the River Ure flows. Wensleydale is named, not after the main river which flows through it as with other Dales, but from the village of Wensley some miles downstream. In the Yorkshire Dales the term 'pot-hole' has become synonymous with cave systems containing vertical pitches, but it is more correctly applied to round holes produced in stream beds by stones swirled around in the current. The flat rock beds below the Lower Falls at Aysgarth contain some fine examples.

2 *Yore Mill*

The large building by the bridge at Aysgarth is Yore Mill, built in the nineteenth century on the remains of an earlier mill damaged by fire. It is now the premises of the Yorkshire Museum of Carriages and Horse Drawn Vehicles.

Opposite *The Lower Falls at Aysgarth*

3 Bolton Castle

The large and spectacular castle seen directly ahead as you cross the fields from Hollin House is Bolton Castle. Built between 1375 and 1399, in a period of intense castle-building brought about by threat of invasion from French and Scots, by Richard Lord Scrope, Chancellor to Richard II, it is regarded as one of the finest extant examples of a courtyard castle. The extent of its interior layout clearly indicates that it was built as a spacious residence as well as for defensive purposes. The central courtyard is formed by a high curtain wall linking four rectangular towers each nearly 100 feet (30 m) high; two smaller towers are placed midway on the north and south sides. The curtain wall is three stories high and the main towers five stories, giving a total of about 70 rooms.

Mary, Queen of Scots was imprisoned there for six months from July, 1568 before being moved to Tutbury Castle in Staffordshire; during the Civil War it was besieged for more than a year by Parliamentary forces before surrender. Partly dismantled after the Civil War it has since been somewhat restored and is open to the public.

4 The Leyburn-Hawes railway

The disused railway track crossed on the return leg of the route was a branch line from Leyburn (reached by railway in 1855) to Hawes where it connected with a branch of the Settle–Carlisle railway operated by the Midland Railway Company. The line was constructed by the North Eastern Railway Company and opened for traffic as far as Hawes in 1878. It served the northern dales for many years for the carrying of quarry stone, dairy products such as milk, butter and cheese, tourists and even war supplies during the two World Wars. There were five stations: Wensley, Redmire, Aysgarth, Askrigg and Hawes. All these stations were closed to passenger traffic in 1954 and the last three to goods in 1964. The metals westwards from Redmire were lifted and the station properties disposed of, but the line to Redmire retained for the use of the Redmire Limestone Quarry Company.

The old line is private property except at Aysgarth where a section of the line can be visited. The cafeteria, toilets and house by the National Park Centre were railway cottages and the disused railway station can be seen across the bridge. The entrance to the track is up the steps directly across the car-park from the National Park Centre.

1·3

CLAPHAM BECK TO INGLEBOROUGH CAVE

A delightful walk through beautiful woods by Clapham Beck as far as Ingleborough Cave. The return is along a green lane on higher ground. Most of the route coincides with the National Park Nature Trail No. 3, described in a pamphlet obtainable from the Information Centre in Clapham.

ROUTE DESCRIPTION (Map 3)

Leave the car-park past the National Park Centre and turn R in the road. After a few yards, cross the river over a footbridge, turning R in the road on the opposite side. Walk up the road by the stream to a L-hand bend. Immediately after the bend turn R through a gate. You are now entering private grounds and a small payment must be made at the cottage ahead.

STARTING AND
FINISHING POINT
Clapham National
Park Centre and
car-park
(98-745692)

LENGTH
3½ miles (5.5 km)

ASCENT
500 feet (150 m)

25

Turn R at the cottage and go along a clear path through a wall gap and then a small gate. The path bends back half L and then back half R (where a path comes in from the L), further along. Climb up a small hill to a junction of paths. Take the wide path to the L which goes along the L shore of the lake. No difficulty will now be found in following this very clear path through attractive woods. After about 1 mile (1.6 km) go through a small gate into open country. Continue along the path for a further 400 yards (370 m) to Ingleborough Cave *(1)*.

Return along the path back to the small gate. Do not go through but instead drop down L to a footbridge. Cross and climb up the field keeping a wall on your L. At the top cross a ladder stile into a walled lane. Turn R down the lane. Further along, the lane descends and then ascends again by a wood to a T-junction, here turn R. Follow the lane as it descends through two short tunnels *(2)* to reach the road by the church in Clapham. Turn L and walk down the road back to the car-park where you started the walk.

1 Ingleborough Cave

This is one of three show caves within the area of the National Park, the others being White Scar Cave on the B6255 road $2\frac{1}{2}$ miles (4 km) from Ingleton towards Hawes, and Stump Cross Caverns 4 miles (7.25 km) west of Pateley Bridge.

Prior to 1837 no more than about 70 feet (20 m) of the cave had been explored, as far as a stalagmite barrier and pool which barred further progress. In that year the barrier was broken down on the orders of the owner of that time thus draining the pool and allowing further exploration to be made. More recently cave-diving techniques have enabled the system to be still further extended to give a link with Gaping Gill (see page 65). The stream-opening a few yards from Ingleborough Cave is known as Beck Head and joins with it through a series of flooded sections.

Ingleborough Cave was first opened to tourists in 1838 and has continued to be popular ever since. Parties are guided underground for about $\frac{1}{3}$ mile (0.5 km) daily from March to October.

2 Ingleborough Hall

The large house on the west side of Clapham is Ingleborough Hall, home of the Farrer family for many years.

Originally the building was a farmhouse, converted first into a shooting lodge and then into the Hall between 1820

Opposite *Clapham*

27

Ingleborough Cave

and 1830. The two tunnels traversed on the return leg of the route were built over Thwaite Lane about the same time for the convenience of the occupants of the house and also to preserve the right of way. Clapham village itself was also considerably altered with the destruction of the vicarage and tithe barn, and the lake seen along the way formed by damming Clapham Beck. The church of St James was completely rebuilt in 1814 except for the tower.

Reginald John Farrer (1880–1920) was the most famous member of the family. Renowned as a botanist, writer and traveller he introduced many new plant species into the grounds of Ingleborough Hall and elsewhere.. The specimens of *Carpinus turczaninowii* in the famous gardens at Highdown in West Sussex, for example, were raised from seed collected by Farrer in 1914. He died in 1920 in Burma.

The Hall is now a residential Outdoor Education Centre for the use of children from a number of Yorkshire Authority areas.

1·4

The Waterfalls Walk

The adjacent valleys of the Twiss and Doe to the north of Ingleton narrow in places to impressive gorges and hold high and magnificent waterfalls. The Waterfalls Walk (sometimes called the Ingleton Glens Walk) follows a circular route in the best of the two valleys. It is one of the most popular walks in the Dales, rightly regarded as a local classic. The walk follows the Twiss upstream to above Thornton Force, then crosses over to the Doe which is then followed downstream and back to Ingleton. The paths in the two valleys have been extensively re-surfaced giving them a somewhat artificial character. In no way does this detract from the route however, for it is superb throughout and few others — if any — can match it for sustained interest. At some points the path is unfenced and runs above considerable drops; care is therefore essential, particularly with children. A small charge is made for admission.

STARTING AND
FINISHING POINT
Ingleton
(98-695733)

LENGTH
4 miles (6.5 km)

ASCENT
550 feet (170 m)

Route Description (Map 4)

From the church in Ingleton take the road which drops down steeply to a bridge. Continue along the road soon crossing a second bridge. (The two rivers crossed by the bridges are the Doe and Twiss respectively which meet a short distance to the south-west.) Immediately after the second bridge, where the road bends L, go R through a gate. Pass the café to a small hut, just before the old railway embankment (1).

Continue ahead through the gap in the embankment and cross the car-park to the far end. From there, follow the clear path which leads through small gates along the gorge of Swilla Glen and through lovely woods, keeping to the L of the river throughout. After about $\frac{3}{4}$ mile (1.2 km) cross the stream over a footbridge (Manor Bridge) and continue along the opposite bank of the stream, to re-cross after a bend by a second footbridge (Pecca Bridge). Just ahead of this footbridge are the first waterfalls (Pecca Falls) set in spectacular rock-scenery. The path continues on the L bank up steep steps past Pecca Falls and a

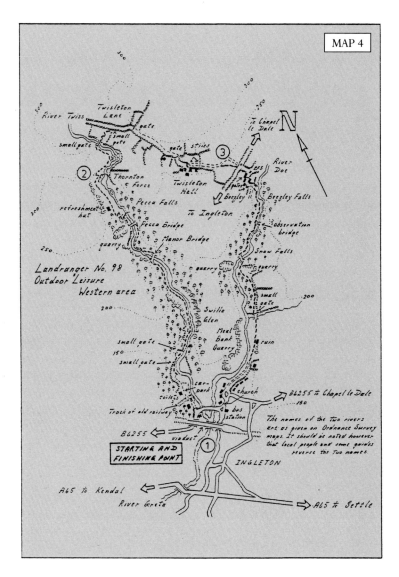

MAP 4

refreshment hut to a further waterfall, Thornton Force *(2)*. This is by far the largest and most interesting of the waterfalls along the route. Continue past the Force to a third footbridge (Ravenray Bridge).

Cross and climb the steps ahead up the hill to a small gate in the top R-hand corner of the field. In the walled lane beyond (Twisleton Lane) turn R and follow it to a farm (Twisleton Hall). Go past barns and through the stile by a gate to the L of the house. Follow the farm road through a further stile and down to a road *(3)*. Take the lane opposite, soon turning R in front of a farmhouse (Beezley Farm — refreshments). Go past the farmhouse to a gate and along the farm road to a second gate.

Opposite Thornton Force

30

Immediately after the second gate turn down L to reach a river (the Doe) by a waterfall (Beezley Falls).

Follow downstream on the very obvious path keeping to the R bank. As a spectacle this is easily the most impressive part of the route, for the path follows a deep ravine past white falls, brown watershoots and dark, sinister pools of deep water. In one place an observation bridge has been erected across the gorge to give a breathtaking and unforgettable view of the ravine at its most savage point.

Much lower down, cross over a second footbridge to the opposite bank and follow the path as it leaves the stream to the L. Continue along the obvious path past a quarry and through woods to a small gate, then beyond over more open ground to a road. Follow this back to Ingleton.

1 *Railways at Ingleton*
The large viaduct crossing the Greta to the south-west of the village centre carried the now disused railway line over the river, the old railway station being at the south-eastern end. The embankment immediately after the small hut at the entrance to the Waterfalls Walk carried a branch line from the main track to Mealbank Quarry which is passed towards the end of the walk.

2 *Thornton Force*
The Pecca Falls are a series of magnificent cascades, Thornton Force by comparison is a mad torrent of white water falling in one tremendous leap into a plunge pool below. Its open situation, directly opposite the footpath as it curves to the right above the small refreshment hut, is ideal, for the Force is both a spectacle and one of the most interesting and well-known geological features in Britain. It is also a place to stir the imagination. The upper part of the rock-face of the fall is of grey, horizontal limestone, the lowest part of vertical and greenish Ingleton slates. Separating the two is a thin conglomerate of smoothly rounded pebbles cemented together. It is the site of an ancient pebble beach over which the sea washed some time between 350 and 500 million years ago. Later the beach was covered by shallow seas and deposited organic remains formed the overlying limestone layer. The junction of the limestone and slate is called an unconformity — the rocks above were not laid down in succession to those below, but instead there is a gap in the time scale of origin caused by the erosion of intervening layers of rock.

3 *Skirwith Quarry*
    The large quarry, seen across the Doe Valley as you descend
    towards it, is Skirwith Quarry worked for gritstone by Amey
    Roadstone Company, a member of the Gold Fields Group.
    The rock, which is very hard and abrasion resistant, is used as
    a road surface aggregate and railway ballast.

*The Twiss below
Manor Bridge*

1·5

To Hardraw Force

STARTING AND
FINISHING POINT
The National Park
Centre and car-
park at Hawes
(98-876899)

LENGTH
4¾ miles (7.5 km)

ASCENT
350 feet (110 m)

Hardraw Force is the highest unbroken fall in Britain; much less well-known or visited are the upper falls set in sylvan woods. This walk is unique in that it includes a compulsory traverse of The Green Dragon public house. Not surprisingly, it is one of the most popular walks within the Park.

ROUTE DESCRIPTION (Map 5)

Go on to the old platform (*1*) behind the National Park Centre and cross the track at the bridge end. Turn R along the far platform and then L up to the road. There turn R. About 100

34

yards (90 m) from the bridge go L through a small gate and follow a paved path through two fields to rejoin the road further along. Turn L over a bridge and past a small cricket field. When the road starts to climb, immediately after a belt of trees, go L up some steps and through a stile (PW sign). Follow the path by the wall along the bottom edge of the field. Little or no difficulty should now be found in following the clear path (much of it paved) which goes in an almost straight line through a series of stiles to Hardraw. Reach the road opposite the church and The Green Dragon.

Old Bridge near the Ure. Hawes can be seen in the distance.

Hardraw Force *(2)* can only be reached through The Green Dragon on payment of a small fee. From the rear of the public house go along a path to the R of the river. After viewing, return to the front of the public house.

Leave Hardraw down the R-hand side of the public house through the small paved yard of a cottage. Climb up the field beyond to a small gate and up the next field to a stile L of a house (West House). In front of the house turn L and follow the farm road as far as a road, there turn L. Where the road bends R go straight ahead down a walled path to a footbridge *(3)*. Cross and follow the stream on its L bank past several small falls to a further footbridge. Cross and return on the opposite side back to West House.

Back at the house turn L between the house and a barn and follow a path to a stile to the R of a further barn. Cross the next field to enter a lane. Turn R to road, there turn L. After 25 yards (23 m) turn R over a stile. Go half L to a farm road and gate and beyond by a large barn leave the farm road half L again to a further stile. The path goes in a straight line over a number of stiles and gates (on my count thirteen!) towards Sedbusk.

In the last but one field before the village, turn R immediately after the stile along a path to a stile in the far corner. This leads into a road. Cross the road half R to another stile and descend the field beyond past a barn to a lower stile. Continue in the same general direction over two further fields to reach a lower road. Again, cross to a stile opposite and descend past a house to the bottom R-hand corner of the field. Continue to descend over an old bridge and into a road. Turn L and retrace your steps back to Hawes.

1 *The Wensleydale Railway*
The station at Hawes was built as a joint station between the Midland Railway Company's branch line from Garsdale (then called Hawes Junction) and that of the North Eastern Railway Company's line from Leyburn, the linkage being completed in 1878. It remained open until 1964 when the entire line between Garsdale and Redmire was closed. The state of the station buildings, platforms and trackway rapidly deteriorated, and it was fortunate that they were taken over by the National Park Authority. The main station building is now used as a National Park Centre, the goods warehouse and office have become the Upper Dales Folk Museum and the station yard is a car-park, whilst the waiting room on the far platform is a warden's workshop. The house to the left of the car-park entrance was the Station Master's residence.

2 *Hardraw Force*
The slopes of Wensleydale are characterized by near-horizontal banks of relatively hard-wearing limestone of the Yoredale Series which produce superb waterfalls where side streams flow over them. The Force at Hardraw was produced in this way by the water of a beck flowing over a limestone scar resting upon softer shales. The light-grey horizontal

Opposite *Hardraw Force*

36

bands of limestone are obvious as are the much darker shales at their base. In the course of time the stream has eroded back considerably into the hillside to produce the ravine, and the greater erosion of the shales has formed a bank under the overhangs of limestone.

The thunder of the Force can be heard long before you reach it, but a sight of the fall is delayed until the final yards. Even so, the great drop of brownish water nearly 100 feet (30 m) high set in its amphitheatre of high cliffs is extremely impressive; the cloak of trees removing from the scene that bareness and austerity that is characteristic of Gordale.

The gorge was the scene during the nineteenth century and again in the 1920s for brass band contests and the old bandstand can be seen on the left just after the footbridge; on the hillside opposite are the tiers cut for spectators. These contests were revived recently, but have now been discontinued once more.

3   *Shaw Gill Wood*

Above the Force, this is largely neglected compared with the Force itself, but it is a delight not to be missed if a few extra minutes can be found for a diversion away from the main route. Neither of the two main waterfalls approaches the Force as a spectacle, but their setting is much superior.

In the Yorkshire Dales National Park, as elsewhere, teams of public-spirited people — mainly young people — have given up much of their free time so that the countryside should be the pleasanter for others. Duke of Edinburgh Award Scheme Volunteers assisted in the restoration of the paths at Shaw Gill in August, 1980 and the top footbridge was built by the Army Apprentices College, Chepstow, in October, 1979.

1·6

UPPER WHARFEDALE

Buckden, Cray and Hubberholme form a compact group of villages in Upper Wharfedale which are linked together in this short circular walk. It is probably best done in an anti-clockwise direction so that the climbs are gradual. The paths from Buckden to Cray and on to Scar House above Hubberholme are high on the hillside giving magnificent views over the Dale. The way back to Buckden is by the river and uses a section of the Dales Way, a long-distance footpath from Ilkley to Bowness-on-Windermere.

STARTING AND
FINISHING POINT
Buckden car-park
(98-942774)

LENGTH
4¾ miles (7.5 km)

ASCENT
500 feet (150 km)

ROUTE DESCRIPTION (Map 6)

Leave the car-park at Buckden through a gate at the opposite end from the toilet block (there is a PFS 'Buckden Pike/Cray High Bridge' by the gate). Follow the clear path which climbs slowly up the hillside. Above a wood (on your L) reach a gate and continue with a wall on your L through two further gates. Shortly afterwards, where the wall bends L, continue in the same direction to another gate. 60 yards (55 m) after this turn L through a small gate in the wall (PFS 'Buckden/Cray/Cray Bridge') and follow a path down the hillside to the small hamlet of Cray, crossing a ford to reach the road near the White Lion Inn.

Cross the road and go up the farm road to the R of the inn. At the rear of the inn take the R-fork at a junction and rise to a gate to the R of a barn. Go through a gate to the R of the next barn, and continue along a lane between walls to a third gate to the R of still another barn. Follow the farm road through two more gates. Cross the field beyond to a gate L of a barn and then bend R following a wall to a footbridge.

Continue half L from the footbridge and then along the top of a small scar with beautiful views of Wharfedale over to the L. (There is no footpath along this section, but the route is indicated by occasional yellow waymarks.) Cross a gap in a wall about 25 yards (23 m) R of the far L-hand corner of the field;

Buckden and Upper Wharfedale

MAP 6

then continue in the same direction keeping a wall on your L to reach the farm of Scar House. By the farm at a PFS drop down to a gate on the L. Bend R then L around the R-hand side of the farmhouse to the farm road. Follow the farm road down to eventually reach the road by the church at Hubberholme (if you have a few minutes to spare, visit this charming Dales church which has a rare rood loft dated 1558 and a superb Norman arch).

Hubberholme Church and The George Inn

Cross the bridge and turn L in front of the inn. Follow the road past a large house on your R (Grange Farm) and a barn on your L. At the end of the next field on the L after the barn go through a gate on the L (PFS 'Buckden Bridge'). Follow the path with a wall on your L to the river and then along the river bank to eventually rejoin the road. Turn L over the bridge back to Buckden and the car-park.

Opposite *Hubberholme Church: rood loft*

GORDALE SCAR AND MALHAM COVE

STARTING AND
FINISHING POINT
Malham National
Park Centre car-
park
(98-900627)

LENGTH
4¾ miles (7.5 km)

ASCENT
650 feet (200 m)

Gordale Scar, a magnificent ravine with overhanging walls 150
feet (45 m) high, is rivalled only by Malham Cove as the most
impressive sight in the Yorkshire Dales. This route includes
both. Waymarks have been placed throughout. A short and easy
but superb walk in magnificent limestone country. Janet's Foss
and Little Gordale, also on the route, would be worth a visit on
their own account, but on this route are dwarfed in comparison
with the Cove and Scar.

ROUTE DESCRIPTION (Map 7)

Leave the car-park in Malham *(1)* and turn L down a minor road
past the Information Centre. At the road turn L again. Opposite

Opposite *Gordale
Scar*

Sparth House, which is just before the Buck Inn, turn R and cross the stream over a small footbridge. On the far side turn R and walk downstream. Soon, cross a stile and then follow the path across two fields to reach a ladder stile in a wall corner. Immediately after the ladder stile bend L with the wall and go through a gap just before a barn. Follow the wall (which is now on your R), soon crossing a ladder stile into a lane.

Go ahead for 25 yards (23 m) to a further ladder stile. Cross and follow the clear path by a wall to reach still another ladder stile just past a barn. Beyond, follow the path to the L of a stream, then follow a wall to twin ladder stiles, and finally continue on through a beautiful ravine (Little Gordale) to reach a waterfall, Janet's Foss (2). The path goes up to the L to a road.

Turn R along the road. Immediately after a bridge and bend in the road go L through a small gate. The way ahead is now obvious, along a very clear path as far as the lower waterfall within the great ravine of Gordale Scar (3). Do not attempt to go further up the ravine, but instead retrace your route back to the road and turn R. After the bend go R over the old bridge and immediately R again over a ladder stile.

Go half L to a wall corner and climb the hill ahead keeping by the wall. At the top (4) cross a ladder stile and go half R to a second ladder stile. Here, turn L on a grassy path keeping the wall on your L. Pass through a small gate (notice the dry valley to the R) and keep in the same direction with the wall. After a barn where the wall bends L leave the wall to continue in the same direction across open ground to reach a road.

Cross the road, go over the ladder stile opposite and along a path half R which leaves the walls to L and R. Eventually you will reach the wall again on your L at a corner where the path forks. Take the L fork which descends to a gate in a wall. The edge of the Malham Cove precipice (5) will now be obvious a short distance to your L. (This edge is not fenced and should be approached with great care.)

Cross the limestone pavements keeping well to the R of the cliff edge to reach a ladder stile on the far side. Cross and descend L on a clear path. Lower down below the cliff turn L with the path heading directly towards the stream. Near to the stream the path bends to the R. (It is worthwhile making a short detour here to the L to the foot of the Cove where the stream emerges.) Follow the path keeping to the R side of the stream to eventually reach a road (6). Turn L and follow the road back to Malham. Or better still, go L over the stile from the road immediately after Beck Hall and follow a secluded footpath on the R bank of the stream back to the centre of the village.

1 *Malham* See page 18
2 *Janet's Foss*
   The small but delightful waterfall of Janet's Foss, and the wooded limestone gorge of 'Little Gordale', make a fitting introduction to the much greater glories of the Scar itself. 'Foss' is an old Norse word for waterfall whilst Janet was reputedly the queen of the local fairies who lived in the cave behind the fall. The original rock face responsible for the waterfall now lies behind a screen of tufa, a soft porous limestone, built over it by the stream. A good time to visit the Foss is mid-May when the floor of the ravine is covered with a carpet of wild garlic.

3 *Gordale Scar*
   Arguably the two most spectacular sights in the Yorkshire Dales—Malham Cove and Gordale Scar— lie near to each other within one mile of Malham village, both formed in a similar manner by stream erosion back into the scarp of the Middle Craven Fault. But there the similarity ends. The glories of the Cove are an obvious feature before you as you approach along Malham Beck. The glories of Gordale by contrast are hidden away, to be revealed only at the last moment when the walker turns the corner into the extremity of the gorge. The huge overhanging walls of Great Scar Limestone, the deep shadow, the chill and the menace of the great ravine of Gordale impress all who go there.

   It is likely that the ravine is a collapsed cave system, the stream originally disappearing down a swallow hole on the moor beyond. The rock step by the lower fall, which is climbed on Route 15, was once extensively covered with tufa, although this is now being rapidly worn away.

   Some very hard rock-climbing has been seen upon the walls of Gordale. The first major route completed was the West Face Route in 1954 by D. Farley and N. Rhodes; this is a very severe route of 220 feet (70 m) which goes up the right wall of the ravine just above the lower waterfall. There are now about 130 routes on the Scar covering all the main faces.

4 *Lynchets*
   An obvious feature of the Malham area, particularly to the east and west of Malham Beck, are the series of giant terraces or steps, each 100–200 yards (90–180 m) long, cut into and across the hillsides. They are called lynchets, a feature to be found both in other parts of the Dales and outside it in areas

47

such as Cambridgeshire and Dorset. The ones in the Malham area were cut by Anglian farmers in the eighth century to produce the extra food needed by the growing villages, when the more suitable land in the valleys had been fully exploited. The terraces, made by clearing and then levelling the ground, were essential for the teams of oxen used in ploughing which otherwise were unmanageable on steep hill slopes.

5 *Malham Cove* See page 18
6 *Iron-Age field boundaries* See page 20

Malham Cove

2·8

BOLTON ABBEY AND THE STRID

STARTING AND FINISHING POINT
Bolton Abbey car-park (104-071539)

LENGTH
6½ miles (10.5 km)

ASCENT
100 feet (30 m)

Bolton Abbey and Bolton Woods are extremely popular in the summer months. The best time for this walk therefore is out-of-season when the crowds are elsewhere. The ruins and chapel of Bolton Abbey, beautiful woods and the impressive Strid are the main attractions along a particularly lovely stretch of the Wharfe. A straightforward walk, with virtually no climbing, which barely makes the moderate category. Bolton Woods is a conservation area, so please keep to the footpaths. A small fee should be paid on leaving the woods by the Cavendish Pavilion on the return route.

ROUTE DESCRIPTION (Map 8)

Leave the car-park to the R of the toilet block and village hall and walk along the minor road to a junction. Cross the road half L and go through the small gate in the gap in the high wall on the opposite side (sign 'To the Priory'). Follow the path beyond down to a footbridge over the river. On the far bank turn L and after a few yards go R up some steps at a path junction. Follow the path for ⅔ mile (1.1 km) to a road.

Go L along the road, soon crossing a ford over a footbridge. Immediately after the ford take the path on the L going R over a stile to follow a path on the R bank of the river. Cross a minor road by a bridge (refreshments are available at the Cavendish Pavilion on the opposite bank) and continue along the path on the R bank of the stream, soon reaching a road. Go L along the road, over a small bridge and then leave it to the L again after a few yards to continue in the same direction along a footpath. Follow this footpath alongside the river to reach the Strid *(1)*. Care should be taken on this section as some scrambling is required. Beyond, continue on the R bank, rising R to a stile after ½ mile (800 m). Follow the path to an aqueduct *(2)* over the river, and cross this to the opposite bank.

Turn L along the path by the river and walk downstream, soon re-entering the woods at a small gate. Follow the clear

MAP 8

STARTING AND
FINISHING POINT

Cavendish Pavilion
(refreshments)

B6160 to Burnsall

Cavendish
Memorial

Bolton Priory

To Halton East

car-park
+ toilets

post
office

To Bolton Bridge   River Wharfe
BOLTON ABBEY

Landranger No. 104
Outdoor Leisure Southern area

path through the woods above the river to reach the Cavendish Pavilion again after $1\frac{1}{2}$ miles (2.5 km); there is a choice of routes along this section, either low down by the river or higher up the hillside. As the woods are private property and contain a number of nature trails, in spring and summer a small entrance fee must be paid at the small hut on leaving the woods.

Continue past the Pavilion and by the river to the far end of the large parking/picnic area. At the end, take a path which goes half R across open ground rising at the end to a stile and road. Turn L along the road past a fountain *(3)* — there are lovely views down to the L over the river and the Priory. After 300 yards (275 m) where the road bends R go L through a small gate. Pass to the R of the Priory church *(4)* and then along the drive curving R to the road. Turn L for the car-park.

51

1 *The Strid*

At the Strid, the Wharfe, which shortly before was up to 60 feet (18 m) wide, is forced through a narrow rock ravine barely 6–8 feet (2–2½ m). The result is a mad frenzy of white water rushing and sliding its way through the gap into sinister black pools below. The rocks on each side are smoothed and rounded by the action of the water, and just near enough to tempt. Attempts to jump the Strid have however cost a few people their lives.

2 *The Aqueduct*

The aqueduct crossing the Wharfe just south of Barden Bridge carries water from the reservoirs in Nidderdale to Bradford.

3 *The Cavendish Memorial Fountain*

The tall structure on the roadside at the top of the entrance to the Cavendish Pavilion car-park is a covered fountain erected by the electors of the West Riding as a tribute to the memory of Frederick Charles Cavendish (born 30 November, 1836. Died 6 May, 1882.) A further memorial in the form of a cross, erected by the tenantry of the Bolton Abbey estates, is in the churchyard.

Frederick Charles Cavendish, son of the 7th Duke of Devonshire, was appointed Chief Secretary for Ireland by Gladstone in 1882. On 6 May, only a few hours after his arrival in Ireland, he was stabbed to death with his undersecretary T. H. Burke while walking in Phoenix Park, Dublin. The assassins were a group of Irish extremists known as the Invincibles. It appears that Burke was the actual target, Cavendish being killed while trying to defend him against his attackers. The murder effectively stopped any attempts to solve the Irish problem for several years.

4 *Bolton Priory*

In 1120 a Priory of Augustinian Canons (Black Canons) was founded at Embsay about 4 miles (6.5 km) to the west of Bolton Abbey. This was moved in 1151 to the present — and much more attractive — site by Alicia de Romilly whose parents had established the original Priory at Embsay. The church and some domestic buildings for the Canons were built in the twelfth century, with further building in the fourteenth, considerably extending the size of the Priory. Work on the West Tower was begun in 1520 but never completed, the Dissolution reaching the Priory in 1539. The Nave of the church was spared and is now used as the Priory Church of Bolton Abbey, with the chancel and transepts

Opposite Bolton Priory

Bolton Woods

forming impressive ruins behind. Recently, a national appeal exceeded expectations by raising £400,000 for essential repair and restoration work on this church which attracts some 200,000 visitors from all corners of the earth each year. The work included the roofing of the West Tower.

The beautiful hall facing the west doorway of the church is Bolton Hall, a private residence of the Duke of Devonshire. The square centre tower is the old gateway of the Priory which was left intact at the Dissolution. The south wing was added in 1720 and the north wing in 1843.

The Old Rectory to the south of the Priory ruins was built in 1700 as the result of a bequest by Robert Boyle to his nephew, Charles, Earl of Burlington, of a sum of money to be used for charitable purposes. The building was used as a school and as a house for the headmaster until 1874, when it became the rectory which it remained until 1978. An inscribed (in Latin) stone on the building describes the bequest. Robert Boyle is much better known for his scientific achievements and in particular for 'Boyle's Law' which was named after him.

2.9

Hawkswick Moor

The great ridge separating Littondale and Wharfedale is crossed by several excellent footpaths, all of them well-waymarked for the maintenance of inter-dale routes is high on the list of priorities of the National Park Authority. The footpaths over Hawkswick Moor, near to the junction of the two Dales, are the shortest of these but, as might be expected, give the finest views. This walk is very popular and, as a result, the footpaths over the moor are now clear and should be easily followed. The route also includes a nice section between Hawkswick and Arncliffe by the river Skirfare.

STARTING AND
FINISHING POINT
Kettlewell car-park
(98-968722)

LENGTH
6¾ miles (10 km)

ASCENT
1500 feet (460 m)

Route Description (Map 9)

Leave the car-park into the road and turn R over the bridge crossing the Wharfe. Walk along the road for 400 yards (365 m) then turn R through a gate (PFS 'Hawkswick'). At a path fork after 40 yards (35 m) go R and continue to rise soon reaching a small gate. Beyond, continue up by a wall to the L of a small ruin, bending R to a ladder stile opposite some trees just after a gap. From the stile the path rises, passing a crag and across the moor (there are yellow waymarks on this section). Continue along the edge of the moor; at the end the path swings half R to a ladder stile on the crest of the ridge. Follow the path on the far side, swinging R at a cairn, and start to descend towards Hawkswick. During the descent, reach a wall on the L and follow this to a gate. Beyond, continue to descend on a good grassy path with a wall to the L, bending L at the bottom into a lane. Follow the lane to a road and, there, bear L to a bridge (Hawkswick).

Cross the bridge and turn R along a lane by the river. By some farm buildings turn R down a narrow lane to a bridge. Do not cross the bridge, but go L over a ladder stile (PFS 'Arncliffe'). Continue on the L-bank of the river over two stiles to reach a footbridge; beyond, cross a further field. Cross the large field following on a clear path to a ladder stile by the river on the far

Landranger No. 98
Outdoor Leisure Southern area
and Northern & Central areas

ARNCLIFFE

River Skirfare

Farracks barn

HAWKSWICK

Knipe Scar

→ N

Gate Cote Scar

descend rift in scar
ladder stile

KETTLEWELL

ladder stile

small pfs
ruin

To Grassington

River Wharfe

STARTING AND
FINISHING POINT

MAP 9

side (thus cutting across a large loop of the river). Go over the footbridge ahead, then R of a barn to a gate. Turn half L across a field to cross the end of a lane by two stiles. Beyond, go to the R of a wall to a ladder stile and then across a field to rejoin the river at a further stile. Follow the path on the L bank of the river to Arncliffe; there go to the R of a large house to a gate in front of a ruin. Cross and turn L along a drive passing the church to a road.

Turn R in the road and walk to a bridge over the river. Cross and immediately turn R through a stile. Follow the stream to a

Opposite Arncliffe,
Littondale

56

Old Cote Little Moor road. Go over the stile on the opposite side and take the path which climbs half R to a ladder stile. Continue up the hill on the path to cross a further stile in a fence. 350 yards (320 m) higher on the path, climb a short face of rock and go over the ladder stile at the top. The path continues to ascend half R crossing two walls at ladder stiles (public footpath signs have been placed at two points where the path bends).

Finally, cross a wall on the ridge top at still another ladder stile and start to descend in the same direction, crossing a wall to the R by a stile after almost $\frac{1}{2}$ mile (800 m) — do not use the gate in the wall passed earlier. Descend in the same direction to cross a crag down a rift (yellow waymarks) and later a wall. Finally, reach the road by the bridge in Kettlewell and turn L for the car-park.

2·10

THE ASCENT OF PEN-Y-GHENT

After Ingleborough, Pen-y-ghent is the most popular mountain in the Dales. Some of this popularity is probably due to its fine name which has a challenging sound about it much in keeping with the mountain itself. Its finest aspect undoubtedly is from the south around Churn Milk Hole, where its bold shape is said to resemble a crouching lion, but it is an imposing sight from any direction. The ascent from Horton in Ribblesdale via Brackenbottom and the subsequent descent via Hunt and Hull Pots is a magnificent walk, although a great deal of work has had to be done on it in order to combat the effect of erosion caused by the number of walkers.

STARTING AND FINISHING POINT
Horton in Ribblesdale car-park (98-808726)

LENGTH
6½ miles (10.5 km)

ASCENT
1550 feet (470 m)

ROUTE DESCRIPTION (Map 10)

Walk from the car-park into the road and turn R. Continue along the road for 700 yards (640 m) to turn L by the village church and cross a bridge. Immediately after the bridge turn L along a minor road; continue along this road to the small hamlet of Brackenbottom.

Immediately before the first building on the L (a barn) go through a gate (PFS 'Pen-y-ghent') and on to a second gate (i.e. the centre one of three gates). After this second gate turn L and go up the hill with a wall on the L. The path follows near to the wall in a long and steady climb up the western flank of the south ridge of Pen-y-ghent, crossing three walls at stiles, to eventually reach the ridge crest at a ladder stile. Cross and turn L to commence the final steep climb. Some scrambling can be enjoyed here, but the path avoids the worst of the rocks by detouring to the R. Above the rocks follow the path to the R of the wall across to the summit *(1)*.

At the summit, cross the ladder stile and descend half R on a broad path to reach the edge of a steep section (cairns). Here the path bends R to descend slowly along the edge. Lower down, below the start of a cliff on the R, the path bends back L by a large cairn. Go through the bend and then take the prominent path to the L descending the moor. Later cross a ladder stile, pass a pot-hole (Hunt Pot) *(2)*, and through a small gate to the end of a lane. (It is well worthwhile making a short detour here to see another famous pot-hole, Hull Pot *(3)*. At the lane end turn R and follow a path through a shallow valley for 350 yards (320 m). The pot-hole is very obvious. Afterwards return by the same route back to the lane end.) Go through the gate to enter the lane and follow this for 1⅔ miles (2.5 km) back to Horton in Ribblesdale. In the village turn R for the car-park (and the Pen-y-ghent café).

Looking towards Pen-y-ghent

60

1 *Pen-y-ghent*

The meaning of the name is still somewhat obscure, although it is Celtic in origin. Among the possibilities suggested are 'hill of the plain or open country' and 'hill of the winds'. The rock foundations are similar to those of Ingleborough: the flat top of the hill is formed by a cap, about 50 feet (15 m) thick, of Millstone Grit, underneath which are the Yoredale Series with Great Scar Limestone beginning at around 1300 feet (395 m). The characteristic 'stepped' appearance of Pen-y-ghent is due to the Millstone Grit and the beds of the Yoredale Series which have worn at different rates, so that the more resistant rocks now stand proud of the hillside. Pot-holes, caves and scars are characteristic features of the plateau formed by the limestone belt. Both Ingleborough and Pen-y-ghent are the remnants of a great rock plateau which originally covered the whole area around Ribblesdale. Rock climbing takes place on the gritstone edges of the mountain.

2 *Hunt Pot*

The sinister slit of Hunt Pot leads directly to a sheer drop of about 90 feet (27 m) followed by a second drop of about 70 feet (21 m). It was first descended in 1898.

3 *Hull Pot*

The opening of Hull Pot is enormous, about 185 feet × 45 feet (56 × 14 m). A stream bed reaches the lip of the pot on the north side, but water only flows over this in wet weather; more usually the stream sinks underground a short distance away to emerge as a waterfall from an opening below the old bed. The water then sinks immediately into the bed of the pot to re-appear at Brants Gill Head north of Horton. In extremely wet conditions, when the outlet passages cannot cope with the excess flow, the floor of the pot becomes covered with water.

Pen-y-ghent from near Churn Milk Hole

2·11

THE ASCENT OF INGLEBOROUGH

STARTING POINT
Clapham National
Park Centre car-
park (98-746692)

FINISHING POINT
Ingleton
(98-696732)

LENGTH
6½ miles (10.5 km)

ASCENT
1850 feet (560 m)

Whernside at 2415 feet (736 m) is the highest mountain within the National Park, but Ingleborough, 43 feet (13 m) lower, is by far the most imposing. To visitors and residents alike Ingleborough is *the* mountain of the Dales. Arguably, the best ascent is from Clapham via Ingleborough Cave and Gaping Gill and the best descent by Crina Bottom to Ingleton, which has a good bus service back to Clapham, and these therefore are the routes described. But on Ingleborough all routes are good.

ROUTE DESCRIPTION (Maps 3, 11, 12 — see also page 25)

Follow Route 3 as far as Ingleborough Cave *(1)*. Continue along the track past the cave and over the bridge immediately afterwards to eventually reach the imposing ravine of Trow Gill. Continue through the Gill to the far end, leaving up a short and easy scramble between sheer rock walls. Beyond, follow a path keeping a wall to the L. After about ½ mile (800 m) — and 125 yards (115 m) after a pot-hole to the R of the path — cross a ladder stile on the L (note that this is not the first ladder stile on the L after Trow Gill).

Follow the path up the moor past several pot-holes to reach Gaping Gill *(2)* — it is extremely dangerous to approach the open shaft — and then up towards the rocky summit ahead (Little Ingleborough). The path is clear except for a short section just before Gaping Gill; some cairns have also been built in the upper parts. Beyond the minor summit continue along the ridge and follow the obvious path up a boulder slope to reach the R edge of the main summit plateau. At the top, the path bends L on to the plateau. Cross to the summit cairn *(3)*.

For the descent, continue beyond the summit in the same direction as you approached to reach a large cairn on the far edge of the plateau. The descent path will be seen down to the L. No difficulty in route-finding should now be found for the path is very clear as it goes straight down the slope, although initially it is both steep and rough. Eventually, much lower

64

MAP 11

Continue on
MAP 12

Ingleborough

boulder slope

spring

Little Ingleborough

cairns

Thack Pot

Fell Beck

Know Gap Sike

Bottoms Rigg

Disappointment Pot

Gaping Gill Hole

Flood Entrance Pot

Bar Pot

ladder stile

pot hole

ladder stile
(do not cross)

Clapham
Bottoms

scramble

Trow Gill

gate

Fosholes

Ingleborough Cave

continue here →
from MAP 3
(small overlap)

gate

Landranger No. 98
Outdoor Leisure Western area

N

down, pass a stream and water sinks on your L and the farm of Crina Bottom on your R. Soon after the farm reach the end of a green lane at a crossing wall and enter it over a ladder stile. Follow for about 1 mile (1.6 km); where it ends continue down over open ground on a footpath in the same general direction to reach a road. Turn L for the centre of Ingleton.

1 *Ingleborough Cave* See page 26
2 *Gaping Gill*
   The great open shaft, 20 feet (6 m) in diameter, into which Fell Beck plunges, is the famous Gaping Gill.
   It is apparent that Fell Beck once flowed through Trow Gill to join the line of the present stream around Ingleborough Cave, for there are dry valleys both before and after

Trow Gill which itself shows signs of water action. The dry pot-holes in the valley below Gaping Gill are the earlier sinks of Fell Beck; it is possible that in the future the flow of water into Gaping Gill will cease as a further pot-hole is opened higher up the hillside. The most convincing place to see all of this is on the final rise to the summit of Ingleborough from where, looking back, the valley of Fell Beck can be clearly seen down to and beyond Gaping Gill. Since the Gill was formed the stream has eroded deeply into the covering of boulder clay so that the valley above Gaping Gill is much deeper than that below it.

Opposite Crina *Bottom on the descent from Ingleborough*

The main shaft falls sheer for 340 feet (104 m), broken only by a ledge — Birkbeck's Ledge, named after an early explorer — at 190 feet (58 m), to the floor of a magnificent chamber 500 feet long by 90 feet wide and 110 feet high (152 × 27 × 34 m). The stream, falling down the shaft, disappears immediately into the floor of the chamber to emerge later at Beck Head Cave a few yards from Ingleborough Cave.

The first successful descent of Gaping Gill was made in August, 1895 by the French explorer, Edward Alfred Martel, the descent taking 23 minutes. Since then numerous expeditions into the Gill have extended the system to a total of about $6\frac{1}{2}$ miles (10.5 km) of passages and chambers, the most important of which have been named. It is thought highly unlikely however that the system is exhausted, with nothing further remaining for future explorers. Of particular interest for some time was a possible connection with Ingleborough Cave, for the furthest reaches of the Gaping Gill system — appropriately called The Far Country and The Far Waters — were within a few hundred feet of the known limit of the cave. This connection has now been achieved.

A winch is erected, by which the public may descend the main shaft, around the Spring and August Bank Holiday weekends. Information may be obtained from the National Park Centre at Clapham.

3 *Ingleborough*

The summit plateau of Ingleborough is particularly rich in remains from the past.

The entire summit, an area of about 15 acres (6 hectares) was originally enclosed by a single stone and rubble wall about 13 feet (4 m) thick made of millstone grit with an entrance probably to the south-west. Part of this wall was unfortunately destroyed in the construction of a summit cairn but much of it still remains. Within the wall many hut circles can be distinguished. The wall was probably built as a defensive position for times of trouble rather than as a centre of permanent occupation. It is the highest hillfort in England and Wales, probably of Iron Age origin, and it played an important part in the revolt of the Brigantes under Venutius against the Romans in the first century AD.

The cross-shaped wind shelter near to the Ordnance Survey obelisk was 'erected by the Ingleton Fell Rescue Team to Commemorate the Coronation of her Gracious Majesty Queen Elizabeth II, June 2nd, 1953'. At the centre and above.

eye-level is a direction indicator to local mountain summits.

    On the eastern side, at the start of the descent to Ingleton, are the remains of a tower built by Hornby Roughsedge, a mill-owner, about 1830 as a house of rest for visitors to the summit. It had a very short life, being damaged on the official opening day by some of the local participants, who were apparently somewhat the worse for drink. The damage was never repaired and the building soon fell into ruin.

The view back from the final rise to the summit of Ingleborough

UPPER SWALEDALE

STARTING AND
FINISHING POINT
Thwaite
(98-892982). Leave
cars outside the
village at some
suitable point.

LENGTH
8 miles (13 km)

ASCENT
900 feet (270 m)

Considered by many to be the finest of all the Yorkshire Dales, Swaledale is remote and rugged with quiet villages of great charm. Appropriately, the Pennine Way follows it for several miles and another long-distance footpath, The Coast to Coast Walk, crosses it at Keld. This very popular route links the villages of Thwaite, Keld and Muker. The first section follows the Pennine Way over the flanks of Kisdon to the west of the Swale and is well waymarked. The return journey is southwards along the opposite bank of the river and then westwards from Muker.

ROUTE DESCRIPTION (Maps 13–15)

Start at the centre of the village facing the Kearton Guest House and the shop (1) (2). Turn R going down a side lane as far as a R-bend; there, go through a stile in the wall to the L by a PW sign. Turn R between a wall and a barn and go through two further .stiles. Immediately after the last stile turn L and cross a field to a gap and then to a small bridge. On the opposite bank turn R and follow a path by the stream; at the wall ahead the path bends L and climbs up the hillside by the wall to a stile at the top. After the stile turn R and follow the clear path which slowly climbs up the hillside. (As you climb, glorious views begin to open up over the dale to the R.)

At the top, meet a wall and follow it to a barn, here the path goes half L to a stile (PW signs). Follow the wall on the L round to a gate; beyond the gate follow the wall on the R as it bends R and along to a farmhouse (3). Go through the gate at the far end of the house and then L through a second gate into a lane between walls (PW sign). At the end, bend R with the wall and then after 45 yards (40 m) turn back half L at a PW sign. Go up the hill to a gap at a wall corner. Continue with a wall on the R. The path now goes ahead across the hillside with wonderful views down to the R into Swaledale. A succession of walls are crossed at stiles, gates or gaps, but the path is clear and yellow

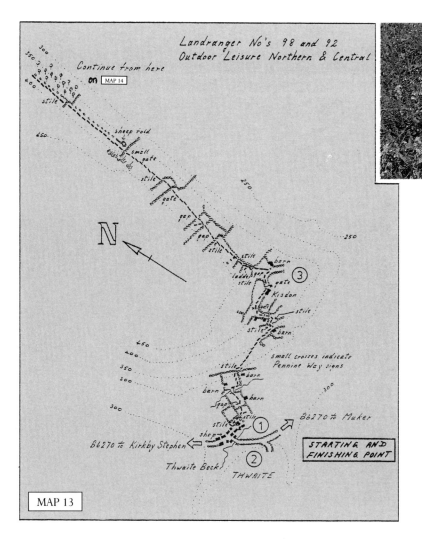

Landranger No's 98 and 92
Outdoor Leisure Northern & Central

Continue from here on [MAP 14]

stile

350 300
400

450

sheep fold

small gate

stile

gate

gap

N

gap

stile

250

stile

stile
barn
ladder
stile

③

gate

Kisdon

stile

stile

stile
barn

450
400

stile

350

small crosses indicate
Pennine Way signs

300

stile
barn

barn

barn

300

gap
stile

300

stile
stile

①

B6270 to Muker

shop

B6270 to Kirkby Stephen ⇐

②

STARTING AND
FINISHING POINT

Thwaite Beck

THWAITE

MAP 13

waymarks will be found throughout. After $1\frac{1}{2}$ miles (2.5 km) (PW sign), towards the end of a long wood on your R, go R through a stile (PW sign) and descend to the R of a small scar. Meet a path lower down and turn L along it, soon to enter Keld (toilets and shop, but no pub) by the church.

Leave by the same path. After 250 yards (230 m) turn down L to a footbridge (4). Cross and go up the path to the L to meet a farm road, there turn R along it soon crossing a bridge. Follow the farm road beyond for $2\frac{1}{2}$ miles (4 km) keeping on or near to the R-bank of the Swale to a footbridge crossing it to the R. Cross and on the opposite side turn R to a stile and then on 45 yards (40 m) to a second stile. Follow the path which now goes half L across seven fields to the small village of Muker. At the village go through a gate and across a yard for a short distance to reach a road. Turn R and walk along the road between houses, at the end turning R to a stile and a gate by a house. (The church (5) to the L is well worth a short detour.)

Go along a paved footpath with a wall on the L. This continues across six fields. In the seventh field the path bends to the L past a large barn to a stile to the R of a further barn; after the stile turn L down a drive to the road. In the road turn R and walk along to a bridge. Do not cross, but instead go through a stile on the R and along the R-bank between the stream and a wall. Cross a stile and then continue on this path over three fields; at the end turn L over a small bridge and immediately R to

Opposite Thwaite

72

a stile. The path gradually leaves the stream to the L over three small fields to reach a further stream. Continue on the R-bank of this stream to a stile and then follow a footpath back to Thwaite.

1 Upper Swaledale

To many walkers Upper Swaledale has a special quality, that is not to be found elsewhere in the Yorkshire Dales. Undoubtedly this is partly explained by its more remote situation in the north of the Park, to which high and wild moorlands, crossed by narrow and unfenced roads of impressive steepness, impose a barrier. Partly, it must also be due to the character of its villages: Keld, Muker, Thwaite and Gunnerside; small compact huddles of cottages — stone-walled and flag-roofed — their position carefully chosen to give them

some protection against the rigours of the northern winter. *The Swale*
'Timeless' is always the word that comes to mind when you
visit them, at their best perhaps on warm summer evenings
when grey-blue smoke drifts from old chimneys and swallows
and martins circle overhead; the music of running water
providing a constant background, for each village rests on a
stream, either on the Swale itself or on one of its tributaries.

In the eighteenth and nineteenth centuries Swaledale was
one of the centres of lead mining, and the mouths of
abandoned levels, hushes, spoil heaps and the ruins of old
smelt mills are a common feature in most of the northern
gills; occasionally, it must be admitted, disfiguring, but
seldom less than fascinating. And, finally, the special character of Upper Swaledale lies partly in its place-names which
are Scandinavian in origin; for Norsemen came into this area
from the west early in the tenth century and, finding it much
to their liking, settled there. Thwaite denotes a forest
clearing, Muker a narrow field, Keld a spring, whilst
Gunnerside was Gunnar's saetr or Gunnar's spring pasture.
Names such as beck, fell, gill and moss are also Old Norse.

2 *Thwaite*

Thwaite is perhaps best known to most as a watering place on the long trek up the Pennine Way. It was also the birthplace of the Kearton brothers, early pioneers of nature photography. On the wall of the schoolhouse in Muker, where they received their early education, two plaques were placed by public subscription: the first 'In memory of Cherry Kearton. Naturalist, author and explorer. Pioneer of wild life photography. July, 1871–Sept. 1940.' and the second '... in memory of Richard Kearton, FZS. Naturalist, author and lecturer. Born 2nd Jan. 1862, died 8th Feb. 1928.'

3 *The Corpse Way*

In the vicinity of Kisdon the line of an old road is crossed which ran from Keld to Grinton through Muker and Gunnerside. The oldest road in Swaledale, it became known as the Corpse Way, because it was the way along which corpses were carried from the upper dale villages to the nearest consecrated ground at Grinton. In extreme cases this involved a journey of about 15 miles (24 km), the corpses being carried in wicker coffins. Muker church was consecrated in 1580 as a Chapel-of-ease to Grinton, considerably reducing the journey, although the first people were not buried there until some years later.

4 *Kisdon Force*

As is the case with Wensleydale to the south, the base of Swaledale was formed in rocks of the Yoredale Series, although in this case at a higher level. The immediate result of this is a superb series of waterfalls formed over the bands of limestone both on the Swale itself and on its tributaries. Kisdon Force is passed on this route, Catrake and Wain Wath Force are a short distance north of Keld, and a further waterfall in East Grain is passed on Route 19.

5 *Muker Church*

Originally built in 1580 as a Chapel-of-ease to Grinton (see above) for the benefit of folk in the upper part of the dale, it was considerably extended in 1761, 1793 and again in 1890. The clock was placed in the tower to commemorate the coronation of George V and Queen Mary on 22 June, 1911.

2·13

THE ASCENT OF WHERNSIDE

As the highest mountain in Yorkshire, Whernside inevitably attracts the crowds, although, in my opinion, both Ingleborough and Pen-y-ghent are superior. The old route up the mountain left from directly between Ivescar and Winterscales. This was always long and tedious, and with the passage of time it had also grown muddy — very muddy. An example of the damage that can be caused by thousands of heavy boots — and many not nearly so heavy — tramping up and down, day in and day out, throughout the year. For that reason, and in order to allow the ghastly scar on the face to grass over, an alternative route (which is in any case immeasurably superior and will therefore give a lot more pleasure) has been arranged by the National Park Authority. It is the route described here — a 'must' for railway enthusiasts.

STARTING AND FINISHING POINT
Ribblehead (98-765793) at the junction of B6255 and B6479 between Ingleton and Hawes

LENGTH
7½ miles (12 km)

ASCENT
1500 feet (460 m)

ROUTE DESCRIPTION (Maps 16–18)

From the T-junction walk towards the railway bridge, turning R along the farm road just before the Station Inn. Continue past the viaduct (1) to a wall at the far end. Follow a path to the R of the railway to the Blea Moor signal box. After the box continue along the clear path to the R of the railway (and later with a stream) to an aqueduct over the railway line. Cross the aqueduct and follow the path beyond on the R side of the stream.

The large waterfall further along is Force Gill. From the vicinity of the Gill take a path which goes away to the R to the R of a fence. Follow this, later crossing the fence at a stile. Follow a path on the opposite side which curves half R across the moor. This later curves to the L and rises up to the summit ridge of Whernside. Turn L to the summit (OS obelisk).

Continue beyond the summit with the wall to your R. After about ¾ mile (1.2 km) descend over two small patches of scree; at the bottom of the second patch by a large cairn go half L and descend steeply to a ladder stile. Continue descending to a second ladder stile and then across a field to a third ladder stile in the far R-hand corner. Immediately after the stile go L through a small gate (i.e. to the R of a barn).

Head towards a farmhouse, passing through a gate and then to the R of barns to a small gate. Continue in the same general direction over four fields (there is a scar and a waterfall to the L) to Ivescar. Go between barns and the house, turning R before the final large barn. Turn L through a gate immediately after the barn and cross the field half R to a gate on the far side. In the next field follow the L-hand wall (crossing a fence) to a stile in the wall corner. Cross the next field to the R to a further stile and

then across the final field keeping by the wall to a farm road. Turn
L. After a gate across the road, turn R over a bridge and follow
the farm road back to Ribblehead.

1 The Settle–Carlisle railway
   The construction of the Settle–Carlisle railway by the
   Midland Railway Company, in the six years between 1869
   and 1875, was a major achievement in civil engineering. The
   aim of the project was to give the Midlands a main trunk
   route from London to Scotland via Bedford and Derby,

which would enable it to compete with its main rivals, the Great Northern Railway which operated the East Coast Route through York and the London and North Western Railway operating a West Coast Route through Crewe.

From the outset it was clear that the forcing of a line through an area of high fell and deep valleys would be a formidable one. Railway lines have to be relatively level, with a rise or fall of only a few feet in a mile, and fairly straight. It was these requirements which necessitated the profusion of viaducts, cuttings, embankments and tunnels which are characteristic of the Settle–Carlisle.

In the 72 miles (116 km) of track between Settle and Carlisle there are no less than twelve tunnels and fifteen viaducts. The Ribblehead Viaduct (originally Batty Moss Viaduct and so called on the Outdoor Leisure Map) has twenty-four arches, is a quarter of a mile long (400 m) and rises about 100 feet (30 m) above the ground; there are also

Opposite Whernside from Greensett Tarn

80

The Ribblehead Viaduct

six others with lengths of about 200 yards (180 m). The longest tunnel, the Blea Moor, is 2,629 yards (2.4 km) long with a depth of about 500 feet (150 m) at its deepest point.

The construction of the line required a vast army of workers who were brought in from all over the country and housed in shanty towns along the line of work. Maiming and death from disease or accident were unfortunate, but common, features of everyday life. In the south porch of the Parish Church at Settle and on the west wall of the small church at Chapel le Dale are memorial tablets to those who lost their lives.

The two most impressive features of the line can be seen from Route 13, the Ribblehead Viaduct and the entrance to the Blea Moor Tunnel. On the moor slope behind the tunnel entrance are the shafts used in construction, and since for ventilation, with adjacent spoil heaps of excavated material.

2·14

CRUMMACK DALE AND THE NORBER ERRATICS

A superb walk, much of it along the lovely green lanes for which the Dales are famous, but the main features of interest are the Norber Erratics and the limestone pavements at the head of Crummack Dale.

ROUTE DESCRIPTION (Maps 19,20)

Walk from the car-park into the road and turn R. Follow the road to the church. Just before the church, where the road swings L, turn R and then L by some gates to enter a lane (Thwaite Lane). Follow this lane uphill passing through short tunnels. At a lane junction at the top of the hill keep R (i.e. continue in the same direction), soon passing a wood. Immediately at the end of the second field on the L after the junction (i.e. approximately $\frac{1}{2}$ mile, 800 m, from the junction) turn L over a ladder stile (PFS 'Norber'). Go half R along a path towards a prominent scar. Near to the scar the path bends round a wall corner on the R to a further ladder stile. (Note here the large boulders from the crag above, which were used in the construction of the wall. The old dalesmen were never anxious to make unnecessary work.) Keep near to the wall until it bends away to the R, then keep in the same direction to a PFS. Make a short detour here by turning L up a small ravine to the open hillside above the scar, the Norber Erratics, i.e. large boulders *(1)* will now be seen over to the R.

Return to the PFS and go L (i.e. continuing in the original direction) across the hillside to reach a wall at a ladder stile. Beyond, go half L to a wall gap and then along a ledge under a scar to meet a wall. Follow the wall down to a lane. Cross the ladder stile opposite and turn L. Go over a stile in a fence and then a ladder stile at a wall. Continue in the same direction (no path) over pasture land, crossing three further stiles to reach a stream by two magnificent clapper bridges. Cross the R-hand bridge and then re-cross over the L-hand bridge (i.e. return to the same side) to the end of a lane (White Stone Lane). Go along

STARTING AND
FINISHING POINT
Clapham National
Park Centre car-
park (98-746692)

LENGTH
8 miles (13 km)

ASCENT
1200 feet (370 m)

the lane to a T-junction, turn R and follow the farm road to the farm of Crummack. Pass the farm keeping the wall on your R. Beyond the farm after a ladder stile take the grassy path which rises slightly L away from the wall. Follow this into the head of Crummack Dale.

After about $\frac{1}{2}$ mile (800 m), at a path junction, fork R along a path which rises to a ladder stile in a short length of wall crossing a break in the scar (Beggar's Stile). Immediately afterwards at a large cairn take a grassy path half L across an extensive area of limestone pavement. (It might be expected

Opposite Limestone *scenery, Crummack Dale*

84

MAP 20

Thwaite Scars

N

Continue back on MAP 19

gate

Long Lane

300

350

Continue here from MAP 19

Crummack

PFS

gate

gate

gate

ladder stile

cairn

1st cairn

rubbish dump

400

Beggars Stile

300

ladder stile

small gate

400

Landranger No. 98
Outdoor Leisure Western area

that this will give slow and difficult walking, but in fact the footpath is grassy underfoot and the very opposite will be found; route-finding is also relatively easy with the aid of cairns.) Where the pavements end, cross a grassy valley and rise up the slope ahead to a small gate. Look back from this point for a magnificent view.

Turn L and follow a track by the wall. The path soon leaves the wall and becomes clearer as it crosses the moor. At a junction go R to pass a rubbish dump. Pass a cairn and 150 yards (140 m) after a second cairn at a further junction (there is a small scar and pavements to the R) fork R. Follow the clear path slowly descending to the end of a walled lane. Follow this lane for 1½ miles (2.5 km) to a T-junction. Turn R and follow back to Clapham.

1 The Norber Erratics

The large boulders covering the hillside above Nappa Scars on the western side of Crummack Dale are the famous Norber

Erratics. Angular in shape and composed of dark grey Silurian gritstone they are obviously alien to the hillside for the predominant rock there is white limestone, clearly seen both lower down at Nappa Scars and in the extensive pavement area some 300 feet (90 m) higher. They originated at a lower level and about $\frac{1}{2}$ mile (800 m) away in Crummack Dale where the Silurian rock bed reaches the surface, and were transported to their present position by a glacier during the last Ice Age, to be left there when the ice finally retreated. The limestone bed, on which they were deposited, has been considerably dissolved away since that time so that some of the boulders now stand on short pedestals of rock, the height of which indicates the amount of solution that has taken place since the boulders were deposited (about 5 cm every 1000 years). Boulders such as these, which have been moved by glaciers and then left behind when they retreated, are called erratics.

Norber Erratics. The dark grey of the gritstone boulder stands out in sharp contrast to the white limestome base rock.

2·15

A ROUND OF MALHAM MOOR

STARTING AND FINISHING POINT
Malham National Park Centre car-park (98-900627)

LENGTH
9½ miles (15 km)

ASCENT
850 feet (260 m)

A superb route, through magnificent limestone country, which must rank as one of the finest walks — if not the finest — in the Yorkshire Dales. Gordale Scar, Malham Tarn and the Tarn House, Water Sinks, the dry valley of Watlowes and the great precipice of Malham Cove are the main attractions, but the walk is magnificent throughout. Somewhat timid walkers should note that a short — but easy — rock climb must be negotiated if they are to continue the route beyond the ravine at Gordale Scar.

ROUTE DESCRIPTION (Maps 7, 21, 22, 1 — see also pages 44 and 16)

Follow Route 7 as far as the lower waterfall in Gordale Scar. Continue up the ravine by climbing the rock step to the L of the fall. Although hands have to be used in the climb, most people will in fact find little difficulty here for the rise is both short and unexposed, and good handholds and footholds abound. Above the fall go half L up to a clear path to reach the top.

Continue to a stile in a wall (PFS). Beyond the wall follow the clear grassy path which goes down a shallow trough between small rock edges and stretches of pavement. After ¾ mile (1.2 km) reach a road. Turn R in the road, but after a few yards leave it to the R along a rough farm road. Continue along this with a wall to your R eventually to reach a cattle grid by a wood. Do not cross the grid, but instead turn L and follow a wall past a wood (to the R) to reach another farm road by a few trees. Turn R over a ladder stile (i.e. to enter the Malham Tarn Nature Reserve) and follow the farm road around Malham Tarn *(1)* as far as Malham Tarn House *(2)*.

Return from the house to the gate at the entrance to the Reserve. After the ladder stile, immediately leave the farm road half R to pass to the L of a small wood. Continue ahead on a grassy path to reach a road by a parking area *(3)*. Here turn R, cross a ladder stile by a gate and then a stream. Immediately

MAP 21

Landranger No. 98
Outdoor Leisure Southern area
Great Close Plantation
600
continue on MAP 22
cattle grid
To Stainforth
600
N
P.F.S.
gate Street Gate
stile + P.F.
Gordale Beck
600
cairn
cairn
stile + P.F.
350
300
scramble
Gordale Scar
Continue here from
MAP 7 (overlap includes Gordale Scar for clarity)
small gate
350
300

after the stream leave the road to the L through a gate and follow a fence up a hill. (To find the well-known Water Sinks *(4)* make a short detour to the L as follows: after about 150 yards (140 m) from the gate take a path half L which soon reaches a wall. Here the outflow stream from Malham Tarn disappears into the ground. After viewing, retrace your steps back to the fence and recommence your climb.)

Near to the hilltop where the fence bends R continue ahead along a clear path over the moor. Just before the descent into a shallow valley (there is a small limestone scar to the R) branch L

MAP 22

continue on Map 1

Malham Cove

⑥

⑤

stile

ladder stile

Lundranger No. 98
Outdoor Leisure Southern area

dry waterfall

small gate

Water Sinks

④

Dean Moor

To Malham

gate

③

To Stainforth

ladder stile + gate

Tarn foot

Continue here from
MAP 21

gate + ladder stile

Ha Mire Plantation

N

①

Malham Tarn

Tarn Moss

Great Close Hill

cattle grid + small gate

②

Malham Tarn Field Centre

toilets

on a faint path which soon grows more distinct. Descend to a wall corner and continue with the wall to your R to a small gate. Cross and turn L to follow the wall down into the dry valley of Watlowes (note the dry waterfall to your L). The path follows the wall through the valley to eventually reach a ladder stile (*important note:* the edge of the Malham Cove precipice, which is *not* fenced off, now lies approximately 150 yards (140 m) directly ahead from the ladder stile. The precipice is sheer — even overhanging — and very high. You have been warned!).

Continue ahead as far as a gate then a stile in the wall on the L (PFS 'Malham Tarn'). Here turn R and cross the limestone pavements (5) keeping well to the R of the cliff edge to reach a

Opposite The dry valley of Watlowes

90

stile on the far side. Cross and descend to the L down a steep path. Lower down below the cliff turn L with the path heading directly towards the stream. Near to the stream the path bends to the R. (It is worthwhile making a short detour here to the L to the foot of the Cove where the stream emerges.) Follow the path keeping to the R of the stream eventually to reach a road (6). Turn L and follow the road back to Malham. Or better still: go L over the stile from the road immediately after Beck Hall and follow a secluded footpath on the R bank of the stream back to the centre of the village.

1 *Malham Tarn*

A major fault line, the North Craven Fault, runs in an approximately east to west direction immediately to the south of Malham Tarn, so that the Great Scar Limestone on the north side is now considerably higher than that on the south. Little sign of this is now apparent on the ground, however, for the limestone face of the fault has been eroded back to its present position at Great Close, overlooking the Tarn; the process exposing the older and non-porous Silurian rocks beneath. It is on these that Malham Tarn was formed. Originally it was twice its present size for the low-lying areas to the east and west of the Tarn, Ha Mire and Tarn Moss, were also flooded. The present depth — at most 14 feet (4 m) — is maintained by an embankment and sluice gate to the south built by a previous owner, Thomas Lister, in 1791.

The Tarn, with its lime-rich water at a height of 1229 feet (375 m), is a highly unusual feature of great interest to naturalists. Appropriately enough it is now owned by the National Trust and managed as a nature reserve by the Field Studies Council.

2 *Malham Tarn House*

The fine house reached at the furthest point to Route 15 is Malham Tarn House, given (along with the Tarn and an adjacent farm) to the National Trust in 1946 by Mrs Hutton Croft. With the purchase or donation of three other local farms between 1964 and 1976 the total holding of the Trust in this area was raised to 3406 acres (1378 hectares). The House, Tarn and some adjoining land have been let to the Field Studies Council since 1947, the House being used as a Field Centre and the Tarn area as a Nature Reserve. Courses are held there between February and November inclusive.

There have been buildings on the site of the Tarn House for several hundred years, but the present House dates at the

most from the eighteenth century. The main part of the *Malham*
house facing the Tarn was built by a Lord Ribblesdale who
used it as a shooting lodge. The eastern wing and stables to
the rear which form the courtyard were constructed by a
later owner, Walter Morrison — wealthy industrialist and
Liberal Unionist Member of Parliament for Skipton Div-
ision — who lived there until his death in 1921.

Many famous people have visited Tarn House in its time.
Of these, Charles Kingsley, who was there on several
occasions and set his famous work *The Water Babies* in the
surrounding countryside, John Ruskin, who left his influence
upon the design of the House, and Charles Darwin, are
perhaps the best known.

3 *The Pennine Way*

This was the first Long Distance Route created by the
National Parks Commission (later the Countryside Commis-
sion). 250 miles (403 km) of glorious walking — most of it
over high and lonely moors — from Edale in Derbyshire to
Kirk Yetholm over the Scottish border. A large proportion
(53 miles, 85 km) of the Way lies within the Yorkshire Dales
National Park. It was appropriate, therefore, that Water
Sinks Gate on Malham Moor was chosen for the official

opening ceremony, held on 24 April, 1965, when the Way was opened at a gathering of 2000 ramblers by the then Minister of Land and Natural Resources, Fred Willey.

Although many people played a part in the creation of the Way there is general agreement the contribution of one man was outstanding. The name of Tom Stephenson, secretary of the Ramblers' Association from 1948 until 1968, will be for ever associated with it.

4 *Water Sinks*

Disappearing streams are a common feature of limestone country; the best-known example occurring just to the south of the Malham–Langcliffe road, where the outflow from Malham Tarn disappears quietly but decisively into the ground, at a spot known appropriately as 'Water Sinks'. It will be obvious however, to all who follow Route 15, that this was not always the case, for the shallow valley beyond, the 'dry waterfall' at Comb Scar and the further valley of Watlowes, leading directly to the lip of Malham Cove, were formed by water action, and mark the old course of the stream which must have produced at Malham Cove a spectacular waterfall nearly 250 feet (76 m) high. Occasionally, in very wet conditions, the stream will still flow further, but a flow over the Cove itself has not been observed since the beginning of the nineteenth century.

It must not be thought however that the stream now emerging from the base of the Cove is that which disappears underground 500 feet (150 m) higher at Water Sinks. Investigations towards the end of last century and more recently in 1972–73 by D. I. Smith and T. C. Atkinson, using water pulses, produced by opening the sluice gates feeding the stream at Malham Tarn, and by the injection of dyes at local sinks, have shown conclusively that this is not the case.

The Cove stream comes instead from Smelt Mill Sink, about $\frac{3}{4}$ mile (1.25 km) to the east, while that from Water Sinks emerges south of Malham at Airhead Springs, the two watercourses crossing each other underground at different levels.

Only under very exceptional conditions, paradoxically in times of drought or heavy flood, does any water find its way from Water Sinks to the Cove.

5 *Malham Cove* See page 18.

6 *Iron-Age field boundaries* See page 20.

2·16

GUNNERSIDE AND HARD LEVEL GILLS

An extremely pleasant walk on excellent tracks over the moorland area to the north of Swaledale. By far the greatest interest, however, will be found in the numerous remains of the lead industry which once flourished in this area. There will be very few whose imagination will not be stirred by the old smelt mills, levels, hushes and spoil heaps which are passed along the way. The route follows Gunnerside Gill as far as the old Blakethwaite Smelt Mill, crosses Melbecks Moor to the east and then runs down Hard Level Gill to Surrender Bridge; footpaths high on the hillside above Swaledale lead back to Gunnerside.

STARTING AND
FINISHING POINT
Gunnerside in
Swaledale
(98-950982). There
is a small parking
space by the bridge.

LENGTH
10 miles (16 km)

ASCENT
1500 feet (460 m)

ROUTE DESCRIPTION (Maps 23–25)

From the parking place cross the bridge and turn L by a café going upstream on the R-bank (PFS 'To Gunnerside Gill'). At the gate to Gunners Gill Hall turn R up some steps and go down a path between two walls, bending L at the end to resume the original direction. Follow the path to the R of the river crossing two walls. Eventually go through a small gate on the R and up some steps. The path turns back half R and then L at a PFS ('Gunnerside Gill/Gunnerside Village'). Follow the path parallel to the river crossing eight walls at stiles or gaps to reach some ruins *(1)*. (An alternative path is available on this section. For this, continue straight ahead from the steps, re-entering woodland; at the end of the wood continue over stiles to the ruin. The route has been waymarked.)

Beyond the ruin cross a stile at a fence corner and go up through a few trees to a wall. Keep on the path by the wall until you can cross it at a stile. Beyond follow a superb grassy path which climbs steadily up the hillside. Eventually reach some ruins. Pass these and continue parallel with the stream across the hillside to reach further ruins, Blakethwaite Mill *(2)*, at the junction of two streams.

Turn R up the hillside (no path) to reach a higher mine road. Turn R along it and follow it across the moor top for $1\frac{3}{4}$ miles

(2.8 km) passing numerous spoil heaps. Care should be taken here in mist or in snow as there are mine shafts in this area which may not be properly covered. Eventually the mine road descends into Hard Level Gill and crosses the stream over a bridge. Turn R on the far side and follow the mine road downstream for 2 miles (3.2 km) past the Old Gang Smelt Mill and Mine *(3)* to reach a road by a bridge. Surrender Smelt Mill *(4)* is only a short distance away at this point and well worth a visit; for this continue downstream along the path to the L of the stream. Afterwards return to the bridge.

Continue from here on MAP 25

MAP 24

450

400

450

500

400

450

chimney
spoil
Old Gang
smelt mill
heaps

peat
store

Landranger No. 92
Outdoor Leisure Northern
& Central areas

③

N

500

spoil
heap

gate

Level
House

Hard Level Gill

550

Moor
House (ruin)

sheepfold

550

500

550

Continue here from MAP 23

Turn R (or L if coming from Surrender Mill) to cross the bridge and climb up the hill on the road, going R at a junction after a few yards. At the top of the hill, opposite a shooting butt, leave the road half R over an earth bridge and follow a fairly clear and level path across the hillside. Eventually, reach a gate in a wall and follow the farm road beyond, soon bending L downhill. Pass several barns to reach a road, here turn R. Later the surface changes to two concrete strips; later still the road bends to the L. At this point, do not go with it, but instead continue in the same direction on a track. After $\frac{1}{2}$ mile (800 m) the path bends half R to a gate; immediately afterwards take a path half L descending to a wall. Continue to descend with the wall on your L to the end of a lane. Follow this lane, soon

MAP 25

FINISHING POINT

B6270 to Reeth · 300 GUNNERSIDE · 350

· 400

berm

berm

turn · berm

250 · gate

· 450

*Landranger No. 98
Outdoor Leisure Northern &
Central areas*

metalled
road ends

N

barn

Bladet · ruin

gate

· 450

250°

Feetham Pasture · 400

300
To Feetham

250°

shooting
butt

Continue here from MAP 24

gate
stiles
Surrender Bridge

To Healaugh
350

Surrender
smelt mill

L To Langthwaite

crossing a small bridge. After the bridge bend L and continue to descend, later with a wall on the L, to reach a farm road by a house. Go down it to a road and then along that back to the bridge in Gunnerside.

1 Gunnerside Gill

The first ruins encountered on this walk are those to the right of the path: these are the remains of an old crushing mill. On the opposite side of the stream is the Sir Francis Level, and Opposite *Old Gang Smelt Mill*

99

the obvious metal cylinder a short distance further along was an air receiver used for operating pneumatic rack and mine ventilating machines. About $\frac{3}{4}$ mile (1.2 km) further along still the path passes by the remains of Bunton Level where there are several ruined buildings with large spoilheaps on both sides of the stream. The hillsides here have been extensively savaged by a number of hushes — ravines produced by lead miners of which the huge North Hush on the western side is the most impressive.

2 *Blakethwaite Smelt Mill* See page 120

3 *Old Gang*

The extensive ruins passed on the way down Hard Level Gill are those of the Old Gang Mine and Smelt Mill. Mining was carried out around this site during the seventeenth century, but an extensive development of them took place during the eighteenth century. The first smelting mill on this site was built about 1770 by Lord Pomfret and his son-in-law (although there was a mill working in the previous century a short distance away); this was incorporated into a second mill constructed in 1805. The mill continued to work until about 1885. Coming down the Gill, there are a number of old levels on both sides of the stream. On the hillside to the left will be seen the pillars and end walls of the long peat store and further along the remains of the mill itself with its long flue rising up the hillside behind. The first mill was sited against the hillside where the flue rises, whilst the 1805 mill was nearer to the path. There are extensive spoil heaps across the stream.

4 *Surrender Smelt Mill*

The ruins, a short distance above Hard Level Gill from the bridge, are those of the Surrender Smelt Mill. The mill was built about 1839 on a site occupied by an earlier smelt mill, and continued in operation until about 1880. The building further along was a peat store and the line of the long horizontal flue can be easily distinguished across the moor.

Note: The remains of the old mines and smelt mills around Swaledale and elsewhere, however unsightly some may consider them, are a part of the history and of the heritage of this region. They deserve our respect. The passage of time will have its own effect upon them, it needs no help from those who find their pleasure in pulling down masonry or in daubing walls with names or trivial slogans. These remains have more than a touch of magic about them, each act of senseless damage reduces it by a little.

Opposite *Gunnerside Gill*

ARKENGARTHDALE

STARTING AND
FINISHING POINT
Reeth (98-039993)

LENGTH
11½ miles (18 km)

ASCENT
1600 feet (490 m)

Arkengarthdale is the most northerly of the National Park dales, running from Reeth to the north-west between the summit of Calver Hill and the imposing line of Fremington Edge. This route runs in a clockwise direction around Calver Hill over Reeth Low Moor, crossing the Dale at Langthwaite, and returning along Fremington Edge. The moorland tracks of short springy turf over Reeth Low Moor are superb, as are the views later in the walk from Fremington Edge, but followers of the television series *All Creatures Great and Small* will be more impressed perhaps by the old bridge in Langthwaite which was featured in the programme.

ROUTE DESCRIPTION (maps 26–28)

From the green at the centre of Reeth turn up Silver Street (B6270) by the Buck Hotel. Walk past the fire station and beyond the houses for 350 yards (320 m), then turn R up a narrow path between walls (PFS 'Skellgate'). Follow this delightful lane through L and R bends to its end at a gate. Continue ahead along a clear path with a wall to the L, contouring the hillside.

After ¾ mile (1.2 km) where the wall bends L, continue ahead to a junction where go L, dropping down by a house (Moorcock House) to a lower farm road. Turn R, soon passing a farm on your L. 200 yards (180 m) after the farm go R at a junction. Soon pass a wall on your L and shortly afterwards go R at a further junction for a few yards to another wall. Continue with this wall on your R. Where the wall bends round to the R, continue in the same direction (no path) soon picking up a path which climbs the ridge ahead. Continue over the ridge on the path which soon becomes much clearer. Follow the path across the moor to a gate by a road (the famous 'water-splash' featured in the television series *All Creatures Great and Small* is just down to the left).

Do not go through the gate, but turn back half R along a very obvious track. Follow this magnificent moorland track of short springy turf between massed banks of heather for $1\frac{1}{4}$ miles (2 km), gradually descending to the road in Arkengarthdale *(1)* — there is just one path junction on the way, at this keep L. Turn L along the road and follow it to the village of Langthwaite.

In the village turn R over the bridge and immediately R again on to the river side. Follow the path downstream on the L bank of the river. After $\frac{1}{2}$ mile (800 m) the path leaves the river to the L through a wood; at a PFS at the far end of the wood go L (i.e.

MAP 27

Continue from here on MAP 28

Landranger No. 92
Outdoor Leisure Northern &
Central areas

Stortiwaite
Hall

N

Arkle
Beck

LANGTHWAITE   sewage
              treatment works
church   toilets   barn

To Whaw
        telephone
        post office   post
        + shop   box   ARKLE TOWN   To Reeth

                              cattle
                              grid

                        ①

                                        Calver
                                        Hill

To Langthwaite

                              barn

                    Continue here from MAP 26

        gate

To Feetham

to Fremington). Follow the farm road to a footbridge by a ford, cross and go to the farmhouse ahead. Immediately after the first house turn L up a lane (PFS 'Hurst'). Where the lane ends continue up the field with a wall on your L to a wall gap at the top of the field. Turn R (PFS) and go up to the R of a hush (a ravine produced by lead miners).

After 400 yards (370 km), at the foot of a large bare spoil heap, turn back half L climbing up a grassy path. The path soon bends R and goes to the R of a second hush. Where this hush ends, continue in the same direction over the moor by some

Opposite Reeth

MAP 28

spoil heaps (no path) to reach a gate at a wall corner. Go through the gate and continue in the same direction along Fremington Edge with a wall to your R. Continue for $1\frac{1}{4}$ miles (2 km) to a stile in a crossing fence.

Do not cross the stile, but instead go through a gate on the R. Descend the hillside on a clear path, later reaching a road. Lower down the road descends through a wood and immediately afterwards bends L with a bridleway (PBS 'Arkengarthdale') coming in on the R. Continue along the road for 55 yards (50 m) more then, where the road bends L, turn R down a narrow path. At the bottom turn R on the road and then almost immediately leave it again to the R at a gate and stile. The path beyond follows the wall soon passing through a stile. Further along cross over another stile on the L and then over two meadows to reach a road near to a bridge. Go R over the bridge back to Reeth.

1 Arkengarthdale

As with those of Upper Swaledale the place-names of Arkengarthdale show signs of Norse settlement. Arkengarthdale itself is 'the valley of Arnkell's (or Arkil's) enclosure', Arnkell being a common Old Scandinavian name, whilst Langthwaite was 'a long clearing'. At the mouth of the Daie the influence is Anglian, however, as shown by the 'tun' villages, such as Grinton and Fremington.

The Dale was an important centre for lead mining, particularly from the beginning of the seventeenth century, the miners living in local villages, such as Langthwaite, Whaw and Arkle Town. Several hushes can be seen on both sides of Slei Gill and there were smelt mills both there and further up the Dale near Langthwaite. Considerable depopulation of the Dale took place in the nineteenth century due to the decline of the industry, with mining families moving southwards to the Lancashire cotton towns and eastwards into Durham.

THE CALF AND THE EASTERN HOWGILLS

STARTING AND FINISHING POINT
Sedbergh
(97-657921)

LENGTH
11 miles (18 km)

ASCENT
2300 feet (700 m)

Although a part of the Yorkshire Dales National Park in the extreme north-western corner, the area of the Howgills is tied geologically, politically and socially to Cumbria rather than to North Yorkshire. It is a splendid region of great whale-backed hills — smooth, steep-sided and grassy (for there is little heather or bracken in the Howgills) — crossed only by lovely green tracks, with superb views both over the Dales and into the Lakes. Essentially, at present, an area for connoisseurs of walking, for the hordes who climb Ingleborough and Whernside, and think them marvellous, have yet to discover it. This is one of the best routes in the Howgills, up the long ridge past Winder and Arant Haw to the summit of The Calf and then down White Fell to Castley. Part of the Dales Way is followed back to Sedbergh.

In cloudy conditions proficiency with map and compass is essential in the Howgills.

ROUTE DESCRIPTION (Maps 29–31)

From the church in Sedbergh take the Kirkby Lonsdale road (A683) past the post office, turning R after 50 yards (45 m) at a junction (sign 'Howgill $2\frac{3}{4}$'). Follow the road up a hill and past some playing fields; 85 yards (80 m) after a telephone box turn R up a lane (PFS 'To the Fell'). Soon reach a farm, go through a gate directly opposite and up a short lane which leads to a further path opening on to the open fell. Turn L and follow the boundary wall for about 200 yards (180 m) then, immediately after a small wood, turn half R up the hillside on a grassy track. Soon reach a crossing track and turn R along it. Follow this grassy track through bracken as it climbs slowly up the flanks of Winder. Eventually, at a cairn, the track swings L and goes up on the L side of Settlebeck Gill to the top of a ridge.

On the ridge meet a crossing track and turn R along it. Follow this very clear and grassy path as it slowly climbs, first on the ridge top and then over to the R; later the path dips into a

MAP 29

spectacular col and crosses it to a fence on the opposite side. Climb to the L of the fence, turning sharply to the R with it later. 200 yards (180 m) from the fence corner at a cairn on the hilltop turn L and cross the open moor (no path) away from the fence to pick up a clear path. Follow this path to the OS obelisk at the summit of The Calf.

Continue beyond the obelisk in the same direction picking up a path after a few yards; follow this to a crossing track and turn L along it. This path goes alongside a ridge and then later descends steeply on its L side. Eventually after a long descent reach a stream junction. Cross the R-hand tributary at a ford and go downstream on a farm road. At a gate cross into a green lane and follow this, later metalled, for $\frac{2}{3}$ mile (1.2 km) to a cross roads. Turn L.

Walk along the road for about $\frac{1}{2}$ mile (0.8 km) to a bridge. Immediately after the bridge turn R through a gate and walk along a minor road past a small church, at a house continuing up the road half L. At the top the road bends L to reach two gates at a junction, turn R and follow a farm road down to a farm

MAP 31

To Sedbergh
(Follow road
for 1½ miles (2·4km)
back to town)

stile

stile

Low Branthwaite

High Branthwaite

gate

small gate

stiles

Bramaskew

Landranger No. 97
Pathfinder No. SD 69/79

barn

N

gates

gate

Nether Bainbridge

stile

gate

gate

Hole House

gates

cattle
grid

small gate

To Sedbergh

Thwaite

gate

gate

Mill House

Howgill Chapel

Gate Side

150

Continue here from

MAP 30
(small overlap)

200

(Thwaite). Do not enter the farm, but instead turn L and then R
between two farm buildings to a gate, here immediately turn L
through a small gate and go along the hillside to the R of a
hedge. Where the hedge bends L drop down to a footbridge. Go
L up the lane beyond, through a small gate and between a house
and a barn into a farmyard (Hole House). At the end of the
farmyard go between the last two barns on the R (two gates),
then turn L and climb to the R of a hedge to a gate. Cross to the
wall opposite and turn L, soon turning R through the first of two
gates. Follow a wall to a farm (Nether Bainbridge), going
through a stile to the R of a large barn and R again down the lane
beyond.

At the end of the lane go through a gate and then half L

Sedbergh

through double gates, continuing to a small barn. At the barn go half L up a hill to a stile and then on to a further stile to the R of another farm (Bramaskew). Continue across the next field beyond the farm to a gate to the R of a small hut, this leads into a lane which goes to the next farm of Low Branthwaite. Go through the gate to the L of this farm (PFS) and over a bridge into a lane, follow this to the last farm (High Branthwaite). Do not enter the farm, but turn back half R at a junction just before. Follow the farm road for a few yards beyond a gate then go half L across the field to a stile. Turn L after the stile up another field to reach a road at the top. Turn L in the road to a T-junction, and then R for 1½ miles (2.4 km) back to Sedbergh.

The Lakeland fells in the distance seen from Arant Haw, Howgills

3·19

TAN HILL INN AND
MELBECKS MOOR

STARTING AND
FINISHING POINT
Keld (92-893012)

LENGTH
18 miles (29 km)

ASCENT
2450 feet (750 m)

A magnificent walk over the great moorland area between
Swaledale and Arkengarthdale. Other walkers may be met on
the southern stretch where the route coincides with the Coast-
to-Coast Walk and to the west where a section of the Pennine
Way is followed, but from Hard Level Gill to The Disputes it is
likely that few — if any — will be encountered. The path is
exceptionally good over most of the route. Old smelt mills at
Swinner Gill and Gunnerside Gill, enormous hushes and Tan
Hill Inn, the highest in England, are on the way.

ROUTE DESCRIPTIONS (Maps 14, 32–36 — see also page 72)

Go to the bottom end of the village and turn R along a path just
below the church and by a small barn (PFS 'Muker'). After 250
yards (230 m) turn L down a path (by a PW sign) to a footbridge
(1). Cross and go up L to meet a farm road. Turn R along it soon
crossing a bridge. Follow the farm road for $\frac{1}{2}$ mile (800 m) to
where it bends L then R with a wall and a barn to the R. 140
yards (130 m) after the barn fork L at a junction.

Go to the L of a ruined building (Crackpot Hall) and up
between a barn and sheep folds to a gate. Continue beyond the
gate on a grassy path across the hillside with a ravine down to
the R; at the end, descend to a footbridge by a ruin (2) at a
stream junction. Follow the path which goes up the L-bank of
the R-hand stream (East Grain). Near some shooting butts meet
a moor road and turn R along it. Follow this for 600 yards
(550 m) until it meets a wider moor road coming in from the L,
there continue in the same direction. Where it swings R at the
top of a huge ravine leave the moor road half L and pick up a
path which soon becomes clearer. The path crosses the moor to
the L of the hush and descends across the hillside into the valley;
it reaches the valley floor through zigzags to the ruins of a smelt
mill (3) at a stream junction.

Cross the footbridge and climb up the hillside ahead to a

MAP 32

Continue from here or MAP 33

③ Sleddowaite smelt mill

peat stone

level

North Rush

Gunnerside Gill

sheep fold

shooting butts

quarry

sheep fold

small hut

shooting butts

stable

shooting butts / East Grain

② Swinnergill smelt mill

Hind Hole Beck

gate

barn

Crackpot Holl

barn

River Swale

N

Landranger No. 92 Outdoor Leisure Northern & Central areas

Continue here from Route 12

MAP 14   (small overlap for clarity)

cross track. Continue to climb (no path) to reach an old mine road. Turn R and follow the mine road across the moor by spoil heaps. After a shooting butt and a ruin on the R, the path crosses a shallow valley then starts to descend towards Hard Level Gill. Where a rough moor road comes in on the R (i.e. by sheep folds and a ruin on the R) turn L on a bearing 344° magnetic, soon crossing a stream and then rising up the moor (no path) to a fence corner.

Continue in the same direction with a fence to your R. After

115

MAP 33

continue from here on MAP 34

x stile

West
Moor

Landranger No. 92
Outdoor Leisure Northern
& Central areas

level

ruin

Great
Punchard
Head

cairn

N

Little
Punchard
Head

small gate

continue here from MAP 32

Friarfold
Moor

cairns

mine
workings

mine
workings

shooting butt

ruin

cairn

sheep fold

ruin

500 yards (460 m) cross the fence at a small gate and follow the path away from the fence over the moor. After $\frac{1}{2}$ mile (800 m) the path turns L at a cairn. From this point aim for the small ruin higher up the stream (you will find it easier if you keep to the higher ground on the L). Cross the stream over a small bridge by the ruin and a level and turn R for 50 yards (45 m), then turn back half L up a path. Follow this clear path (cairns) across the moor and then along the moor edge.

Opposite *Upper Swaledale from Crackpot Hall*

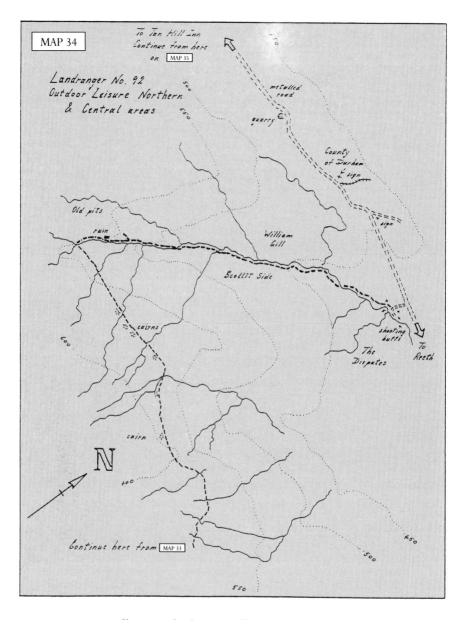

To Tan Hill Inn
Continue from here
on MAP 35

MAP 34

Landranger No. 92
Outdoor Leisure Northern
& Central areas

metalled road

quarry

County of Durham sign

Old pits

ruin

William Gill

sign

Scollit Side

cairns

shooting butts

The Disputes

To Reeth

N

cairn

Continue here from MAP 33

Finally, overlooking William Gill continue in the same direction to reach the stream. Cross, turn R, and follow the stream for $1\frac{1}{2}$ miles (2.4 km) to a road. Turn L on the road and walk for $2\frac{1}{2}$ miles (3 km) to Tan Hill Inn *(4)*.

Take the path directly opposite the Inn (PW sign). Follow the clear path across the moor going R at two path junctions after about 650 yards (600 m). After about 2 miles (3.2 km) reach a gate by a barn. Go along the farm road beyond, where this bends L go ahead to a small gate and continue again across the open moor on a path. After $\frac{1}{2}$ mile (800 m) pass through a gate in a fence and later another gate in a wall. Go along the farm road beyond to a walled lane and down to a farm. Go through a

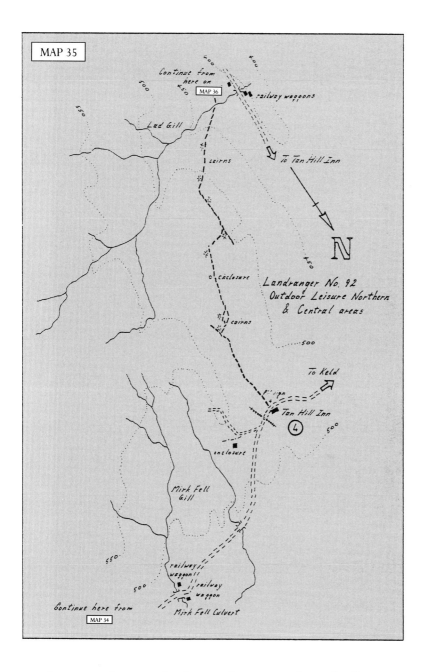

MAP 35

Continue from here on MAP 36

railway waggons

Lad Gill

500

450

cairns

To Tan Hill Inn

N

o enclosure

Landranger No. 92
Outdoor Leisure Northern
& Central areas

cairns

450

500

500

To Keld

Tan Hill Inn

4

500

enclosure

Mirk Fell
Gill

550

railway
waggon

500

railway
waggon

Continue here from
MAP 34

Mirk Fell Culvert

gate between a house and a barn and continue down the farm road. Before it goes over a bridge, turn R down a path to a footbridge. Cross and follow the path up the hillside half R to an upper lane, there turn R for Keld.

MAP 36

1 *Kisdon Force* See page 76

2 *Swinner Gill Smelt Mill*

    The ruins at the stream junction up Swinner Gill are of a small smelt mill which worked from 1769 to about 1820. The mill was a small rectangular building of two rooms; the right-hand room (facing the mill from East Grain) contained the hearths for smelting and the left-hand room bellows which

Opposite Tan Hill
Inn

120

were driven by a waterwheel. The remains of a flue can be seen running up the hillside behind the mills.

3 *Blakethwaite Mill*

The area around Gunnerside Gill is particularly rich in remains from the heyday of the lead mining industry. The head of an enormous hush is reached as you come over the moor top from Swinner Gill and several others are only too obvious on the facing slopes across the valley. The open mouths of levels are passed as you descend and further ruins and spoil heaps can be seen to the right lower in the gill.

The most impressive remains on this route, however, are those of Blakethwaite Mill which are situated at the point where Gunnerside Gill is crossed. The remains of the mill are on the hillside between the two streams with a long flue, cut into solid rock, rising behind. The building by the footbridge, with arches on the stream side, was used as a peat store — the arches giving the air circulation necessary to dry the peat. The mill worked local ores and was in use for about sixty years from 1820.

4 *Tan Hill Inn*

1732 feet (528 km) above sea-level, this is reputed to be the highest inn in England; an important stopping-place for Pennine Way walkers who, approaching over Stonesdale Moor, see it beckoning before them like an oasis with the promise of much-needed refreshment. They are part of a long tradition, for Tan Hill Inn, by the metalled road out of Arkengarthdale and at the crossing point of earlier pack-horse trails, has been serving the needs of travellers for many centuries.

Thin coal seams, low in the Millstone Grit beds, which top the nearby fells, were worked at collieries around Tan Hill from the thirteenth century until last century. (Similar mining also took place on Fountains Fell further to the south.) The coal produced was sent to local towns and in the eighteenth and nineteenth centuries to nearby smelt mills.

A sheep fair is still held by the inn in the third week of May each year.

APPENDICES

ACCESS FOR THE WALKER

It is important to realize that the designation of a National Park does not change the ownership of the land within it in any way. In the case of the Yorkshire Dales National Park, for example, less than one per cent of the land is under any form of public ownership. The laws of access and trespass apply just as much to areas of private land within a National Park as to those outside it.

The National Parks and Access to the Countryside Act of 1949 required County Councils in England and Wales to prepare maps which showed all paths over which the public had a right to walk. The final form of the map is referred to as a definitive map and copies are held at the offices of the County Council and District Council and sometimes by the Parish Council concerned. Public Paths can only be diverted or deleted from a definitive map by the raising of a Diversion Order or an Extinguishment Order respectively. The paths are classified as either footpaths (for walkers only) or bridleways (for walkers, horseriders and cyclists). These public paths were included on the now withdrawn one inch to one mile (1: 63 360) Seventh Series, most 1:25 000 Second Series (i.e. Pathfinder), 1:50 000 First and Second Series (i.e. Landranger) and the Outdoor Leisure maps.

A 'road used as a public path' is a highway, other than a public path, used by the public mainly for the purpose for which footpaths or bridleways are used. They may still be shown as such on Ordnance Survey maps, although they are being reclassified on definitive maps as either footpaths, bridleways or byways open to all traffic. In any event a public right-of-way exists. Furthermore, many unmetalled roads (fenced- and unfenced) which give excellent walking are open to the public, although the Ordnance Survey map does not specifically show them as having public rights-of-way.

Although there are a large number of footpaths and bridleways within the area of the Park, there are also substantial areas where none exists. Fortunately, however, access may also be permitted to such areas under one of the following.

ACCESS AGREEMENTS

Under the National Park and Access to the Countryside Act of 1949, National Park Authorities have the power to negotiate Access Agreements with landowners whereby access is given in return for compensation in the form of a grant. This access may be subject to conditions as appropriate to the area.

NATIONAL TRUST PROPERTIES

The Trust policy is to give free access at all times to its open spaces; however there cannot be unrestricted access to tenanted farms, young plantations and woods, or certain nature reserves where the preservation of rare fauna and flora is paramount.

The public has access to the south-east shore of Malham Tarn which is owned by the Trust.

PERMISSIVE PATHS

A number of footpaths on land in the Bolton Abbey area, held by the Trustees of the Chatsworth Settlement, have been opened for public use, although not in themselves having legal rights-of-way. These are all signposted and waymarked. Information can be obtained from the information kiosk at Cavendish Pavilion near Bolton Abbey.

Access is allowed, on payment of a small fee, to the lakeside path from Clapham to Ingleborough Cave (Routes 3 and 11), to those of the Waterfalls Walk (Routes 4) and to Hardraw Force (Route 5).

TRADITION

Walkers have for very many years walked freely

- keep to public paths across farmland;
- use gates and stiles to cross fences, hedges and walls
- leave livestock, crops and machinery alone;
- take your litter home;
- help to keep all water clean;
- protect wildlife, plants and trees;

- take special care on country roads;
- make no unnecessary noise.

This Charter is for practical guidance in England only. It was prepared by the Countryside Commission.

ADDRESSES

The Camping and Caravanning Club,
Greenfields House, Westwood Way, Coventry
CV4 8JH
Tel: Coventry (0203) 694 995

Countryside Commission,
John Dower House, Crescent Place,
Cheltenham, Gloucestershire GL50 3RA
Tel: Cheltenham (0242) 521381.

Council for National Parks,
246 Lavender Hill, London SW11 1LJ
Tel: (071) 924 4077

The Dalesman Publishing Co. Ltd.,
Clapham, via Lancaster, North Yorkshire.
For books on the life of the Dales.

The Long Distance Walkers Association.
Membership Secretary, 117 Higher Lane,
Rainford, St Helens, Merseyside WA11 8BQ
Tel: St Helens (0744) 882 638

The National Trust,
36 Queen Anne's Gate, London SW1H 9AS
Tel: (071) 222 9251.
(Regional Information Officer,
Miss J. Ibbotson, The Yorkshire Regional Office
of the National Trust, The Goddards, 27
Tadcaster Road, Dringhouses, York YO2 2QG
Tel: York (0904) 702021.)

Rambler's Association,
1/5 Wandsworth Road, London SW8 2XX
Tel: (071) 582 6878.

The Yorkshire and Humberside Tourist Board,
312 Tadcaster Road, York, North Yorkshire
YO2 2HF.
Tel: York (0904) 707961.

Yorkshire Dales National Park,
'Colvend', Hebden Road, Grassington, Skipton,
North Yorkshire BD23 5LB
Tel: Grassington (0756) 752748.
For all orders by post of National Park
publications and for all telephone and postal
enquiries.

Yorkshire Dales Society,
152 Main Street, Addingham, Ilkley, West
Yorkshire LS29 0LY
Tel: Ilkley (0943) 607868.

Youth Hostels Association (England and Wales),
Trevelyan House, 8 St Stephen's Hill, St Albans,
Hertfordshire AL1 2DY
Tel: St Albans (0727) 855 215.

INDEX